# The Effective Computer

# The Effective Computer
## A Management by Objectives Approach

Kit Grindley
*Director, Urwick Dynamics Limited*

John Humble
*Director, Urwick Orr and Partners Limited*

A Division of American Management Associations

Library of Congress Catalog Card Number: 73-79243
International Standard Book Number: 0-8144-5334-1
First American Edition, 1974

Third Printing

# Contents

# Preface

The modern age has a false sense of superiority because of the great mass of data at its disposal. But the valid criterion of distinction is rather the extent to which man knows how to perform and must master the material at his command.

Johann Wolfgang von Goethe, 1810

There is considerable evidence that the computer has already made a significant contribution to business and other organizations, and it is probable that installations will increase at the rate of some 20 per cent per annum in the 'seventies. By 1980, it is estimated* that some 10 per cent of the British working population will be directly involved in supplying or serving computer systems.

Paradoxically, there is also ample evidence to show that many managing directors, presidents, and general managers in organizations with in-stalled computers are disappointed and bewildered. Since many of the promises of a "brave new computer world" are still unfulfilled, it is fashion-able to overreact and accuse the computer of being an expensive confi-dence trick. Clearly, some sensible perspective is needed.

* *Computers in Business* National Computing Centre Ltd, p. 12.

# The effective computer

Our own experience as practicing management consultants suggests that there are still profound misconceptions about the computer and the valid ways in which it can help an organization. This is matched by top management's failure to *manage* the computer and make it truly effective as a tool for business improvement. No matter how well run and efficient a computer department may be in itself, the real benefits and true effectiveness are secured by the users. Effectiveness is getting the right things done; efficiency is doing things right. In our opinion:

Technical objectives *per se* are not worth pursuing—e.g., updating stock records on a computer, the creation of a data bank, the installation of a real-time customer inquiry system.

The only valid objective for computers is to assist in achieving defined business improvements which would be impossible or uneconomical without the computer.

Computer users must be committed to the defined improvements and are ultimately responsible for carrying out the plan to achieve them. The computer department alone can only produce computer systems, not business improvements.

This book is a summary of proven ways to achieve these goals, and it is meant to be read by line managers and functional specialists in organizations in which a computer is installed. Hopefully, it will also be of interest to those about to install a computer and to all students of management.

Although this is meant to be a practical book, it is not a "do-it-yourself kit." Every organization must think through its own procedures and specific methods. The most useful contribution we can make is to provide a new insight into the relationship between general management and the computer. What Stafford Beer said in the preface of his brilliant book *Brain of the Firm** sums up precisely our view:

In communication everything depends on what you end up with, not on what was actually said or written down. Here you are supposed to end up with an insight, not with an agglomeration of facts. When everything is understood the details cease to matter very much, or can be changed, or can even be abandoned for another set.

# A Management by Objectives approach

By definition, a computer-based information system can only be effective when it fits into a wider system of general management purpose, methods,
* Penguin, 1972.

and style in an organization. The general management system we have adopted, Management by Objectives (MBO), has been described by us in detail elsewhere,* but it may be useful to summarize some essential features, by way of background.

Peter Drucker in *The Practice of Management*† gave the classic definition:

> What the business needs is a principle of management that will give full scope to individual strength and responsibility, and at the same time give common direction of vision and effort, establish teamwork and harmonize the goals of the individual with the common weal. The only principle that can do this is Management by Objectives and self-control.

In seeking to interpret the organization's need to clarify and achieve its profit and growth goals with the manager's need to contribute and develop himself, certain important features can be observed.

1.  *A total view* is needed, since the immense interdependence between the parts of an organization is easily overlooked. To computerize one element of the information system should automatically cause us to look at the implications for people, plans, organization structure, and so on. The dynamic nature can be shown thus:

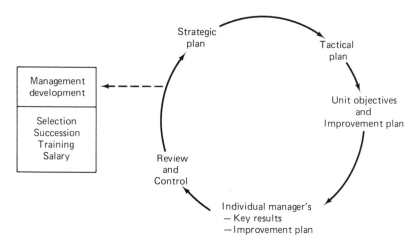

This self-critical examination should not be too introspective. Since the major threats and opportunities lie in the external world, a rigorous

---

\* J. W. Humble, *Improving Business Results*, McGraw-Hill for Management Centre/Europe, 1967; and J. W. Humble (Editor), *Management by Objectives in Action*, McGraw-Hill, 1970.
† Heinemann, 1955.

analysis of customer needs, changing technology, and competitors' activities is a basic feature of making the strategic plan.

2. *Resources and effort should be concentrated* on the small number of key areas and key tasks which have great leverage for success or failure. Against the background of overall purpose, it is essential to be selective: trying to do everything equally well is disastrous for manager and business alike. So, great care is taken to select the key areas in which performance must be maintained at a given level, and those in which positive and specific improvement is sought. Again, a computer-based information system may help us to monitor success in the key maintenance areas and give new information patterns to help us to find and control improvements, or it may release a manager from the burden of managing clerical systems and give him time to think more carefully about new opportunities.

3. *Results, not activities,* are our main concern. Being busy is not necessarily being effective. The information from a computer system is only a "part result"—the real result is when a manager uses the information to secure improvements.

4. Information, whether formal or informal, computerized or not, requires a *careful analysis of the user's needs* and expectations. It must match the selected key areas or it may distract attention into trivial matters. Most organizations have too much raw data and not enough intelligent information: the result is confusion. Self-control, rather than imposed control, should be built into the information system, so that each individual knows directly what is happening and can himself make corrections.

5. *Organization structure* is a means by which the purpose of the business can be expressed to many people. No structure can be thought about sensibly except in relation to purpose and objectives. The formal information flow, computerized or not, must match the organization. In turn, new information capabilities make possible new forms of structure.

6. The *motivation and development* of individuals and teams of managers is an essential part of Management by Objectives. This is particularly true in working together at fact finding and sorting out alternative solutions; building jobs which provide people with maximum enrichment and opportunities for self-expression; using multilevel, multi-discipline teams for innovative problem solving; planning learning experiences to acquire new knowledge, skills, and behavior; developing equitable reward and promotion systems.

The MBO general management approach to this book is, therefore, concerned with major points of principle, built up from the experience of thousands of organizations throughout the world. We have no commitment to any specific forms or mechanistic procedures.

## The form of the book

After a frank appraisal of what went wrong, a major part of the book deals with the involvement of management with the computer experts and their joint work in assessing the present position and strategic opportunities for the use of the computer. The role of project teams in implementing agreed recommendations is discussed, and a program of control and review is proposed. Obviously, the success of these new and significant uses of the computer requires improved management efficiency in the computer department itself. Moreover, it is clear that a major cause of failure in the effective use of computers lies, not in the technical and organizational fields, but with human failures in behavior, knowledge, and skills. A part of this book analyzes the different viewpoints of line and specialist managers, and outlines various means for motivating and training people at all levels. Finally, there is a personal, challenging note for the reader: can your computer be made effective? Questions and checklists are provided to stimulate analysis and action plans.

## Acknowledgments

Since this is a book built on consulting experience, it could not have been written without the cooperation of our clients. Except where a case study has already been published elsewhere and the name of a corporation revealed, we have, for reasons of professional etiquette, kept the cases anonymous.

While they have no responsibility for the final result, we have drawn continuously on the experience and guidance of our colleagues in the Urwick Group. Urwick Dynamics alone has in the last 13 years undertaken over 400 computer consulting assignments in some 20 countries. We are particularly grateful to Peter Bridgman and Tony Dowson for their advice and to Miss Phyllis Cutting and her team at the Urwick Management Intelligence Services.

Finally, we thank our wives for their patience and encouragement. The objectives of writing a book on weekends and meeting with one's family are not easily reconciled.

KIT GRINDLEY<br>JOHN HUMBLE

# Part 1
# What went wrong

## Introduction

Since the early nineteen-fifties, when the computer was first taken over from the mathematician, it has been promoted for business use with skill and enthusiasm. The following figures indicate the trend:

| Year | | No. of installations | | | |
|------|------|------|------|------|------|
| 1956 | | 1,000 | | | |
| 1961 | | 10,000 | | | |
| 1966 | | 50,000 | | | |
| 1971 | more than | 100,000 | (USA | = | 73,700) |
| | | | (W. Europe | = | 24,400) |
| | | | (Japan | = | 6,000) |
| Forecast: | | | | | |
| 1980 | | 200,000 | | | |

**Figure 1.1**  Number of business installations in the world.

During this time, more than a million systems analysts and programmers have been trained and are currently occupied in making these machines work. Including the replacement costs of the earlier machines, something exceeding $48,000 million has been spent on hardware alone. When the cost of programs and systems design, and all the peripheral equipment, is included, we find that in the United States alone, in 1970, around 10 per cent of the total business investment expenditure was on computer hardware and software.

Looking ahead, it is probable that within a decade the computer industry will become, in terms of annual unit sales, the third largest in the world—exceeded only by the automobile and oil industries. In Britain alone, we can anticipate[1] that, even with a reduced growth rate of computer installations, by 1980 more than 320,000 British organizations will be using computers, i.e., approximately 60 per cent of the total number of limited companies in the country. By then, something like 10 per cent of the British working population may be directly involved in supplying or servicing computer systems.

With this background of growth and future promise, one might expect that the great majority of present computer users are thoroughly satisfied with the benefits so far secured. In fact, the management journals and financial press often report on surveys[2] that indicate:

> a majority of users are disappointed with the results obtained from their computer;

> most installations fail to show the expected return on investment;

> in some cases there is a worsening of performance in business areas where the computer has been used.

Typical of cases published in the USA and the UK are the following:

### Case A

► AN AMERICAN COMPANY
One of the top 100 on *Fortune*'s list of the 500 largest industrial corporations in America started computer project after computer project, all of which either failed or cost many times the amount originally budgeted. According to one of the data processing executives, who has lived through several of the debacles, the company has:

> Spent more than $500,000 in two years attempting to standardize accounting and business systems so that they could be put on computers, and got absolutely nowhere.

> Spent $500,000 during the past three years in an attempt to develop a method of identifying and coding common business data used throughout the company without being able to make substantial progress.

> Run through a long list of computer programming projects, costing between $100,000 and several million dollars each, all failures.

This is a corporation whose main business is in advanced technologies. Its management is sophisticated and progressive. The first computer was bought in 1958 and the firm now has more than 500 people working in its data processing department. The annual data processing budget totals more than $10 million: 35 to 40 per cent of it for hardware and installations. The rest, in one form or another, goes for people, most of whom work on systems analysis and programming.

This company is divided into 25 profit centers, each of which has its own computer system. Each of the centers writes its own applications programs for operations that are common to them all—payroll, billing, accounting, and so forth. None of the programs written in one center can be used by the other centers, i.e., they cannot be used on other computers. For a single application, the package of programs costs around $250,000 to prepare, and most packages cause so much difficulty that a long time passes before any one of them is actually put on a computer. This means the computers are underemployed, a fact well known by the managers and submanagers in the various profit centers. Filled with notions of the fantastic things computers can do, they press the data processing department for further computer applications. The data processing department, stuck with the computer mystique, has a hard time refusing. The trickle of applications programs actually reaching the computer is hardly increasing, yet, thanks to the growing number of new projects, the budget for programming is rising by 30 per cent a year.

## Case B

▶ A BRITISH COMPANY
In the United Kingdom, a company high up in *The Financial Times'* top 500 list decided to install a computer eight years ago to provide an integrated accounts system for its 800,000 customers. Computer equipment costing $480,000 was proposed by a manufacturer for this job and accepted by the company. After eighteen months of systems design and programming work, further equipment costing an additional $600,000 was needed. After two more years, the accounts began to be transferred to the machine. Instead of occupying one-and-a-half shifts as originally forecast, the enlarged computer was occupied for four shifts (around the clock, including weekends), a large amount of additional computer processing had to be subcontracted to a service bureau, and even then only 75 per cent of the work could be done. A further proposal was put to the board, involving more than a million dollars' worth of new equipment. During the four years that the project had taken, $480,000 had been spent in systems and programming work. The new system had involved nightmares of reorganization for the accounts staff and morale had fallen to a low level. The time taken to produce invoices and statements had worsened by an average of six days each month; the accounts receivable increased from 2.9 to 4.1 months' sales, involving more than $4 million. Furthermore, a special section of clerks had to be created to deal with customer queries, which had increased by 300 per cent in the four years.

## A paradox

Taken at face value, the disappointments indicated by such cases, and similar findings from surveys, should cause many organizations to remove their computers. Certainly, with the evidence publicly available, one might expect a severe cutback in new investment in computers.

Why, then, do shrewd top managers in the 'seventies analyze their own needs and study other peoples' experience . . . and still go ahead with computer installation? Why, then, is there agreement among observers of the economic scene that the growth of the computer business is a matter of confidence in this decade?

The underlying explanation of this paradox is that, although computers have made a significant and beneficial contribution, there is disappointment and preoccupation with failure arising substantially from *unfulfilled expectations*. The dramatic and revolutionary promises made in the literature and feasibility studies have been unrealistic. The entrancing vision of an "all singing, all dancing," comprehensive, integrated management information system often turned out to be a hard-earned payroll application in year one. No wonder top management feels let down!

The unpalatable fact is that getting a computer into effective action is more expensive and more complicated than the typical optimistic feasibility study indicates. As Peter Drucker once said, "The trouble with good ideas is that they degenerate into hard work."

The blame for these shortcomings was placed first of all on computers themselves, which were said to be too small, too slow, too expensive, and too awkward to use. Later, the computer experts were blamed and accused of pursuing technical objectives and not understanding real business needs. Of late, it has become fashionable to single out "lack of management participation" as the biggest single factor responsible for computer disappointment. Clearly, what is now needed is a sense of perspective. Perhaps the most helpful approach is to accept the computer in an unexaggerated way as a proven management tool, and concentrate on improving its contribution.

By asking, in Part 1, what went wrong, we offer guidance to the many organizations which have yet to install a computer. More important, the history of typical installations indicates fundamental issues—such as purpose, relationship with organization structure, and human problems—which still inhibit the effective use of computers today. Undoubtedly, a major continuing difficulty is the misconception about the true nature of the computer.

## What went wrong—a classic sequence

Urwick Dynamics recently made a comprehensive study of a cross section of disappointed users to see if any significant common features emerged. A classic sequence was identified in four main stages:

1. *A superficial approach to computer purchase and installation.*
2. *Overdelegation by top management.*
3. *Confusion of objectives.*
4. *Cost escalation.*

We will describe these stages in more detail, caricaturing a little for the sake of emphasis.

### Stage 1. A superficial approach to computer purchase and installation

Usually the process started with enthusiasm for a computer by one or more people in the organization—which gave rise in its turn to the search for a logical justification of the expenditure involved. The common justification was that of performing on the machine some clerical process presently done by human beings. It was argued that human beings would then be saved, and thus costs reduced. Since these cost savings rarely justified the expenditure on their own, other business improvements, not measured but classed as "intangibles," were mentioned. These persuaded the board, faced perhaps with only a breakeven case on monetary savings, to go ahead. As an examination of the major uses made of the computer indicates, the financial controller or accountant was frequently the enthusiast who got things started.

A feasibility study was made, invariably in close cooperation with a computer manufacturer who, of course, had every right to make out the best possible case for installation. Perhaps this was inevitable, since a company considering the installation of a computer seldom had managers of its own with adequate depth and breadth of knowledge about the computer and its problems. If it had been a new machine tool, a new truck, or a new typewriter, there would have been a backlog of experience which would have enabled top management to ask the right searching questions, to compare alternative solutions, and to put the project into a wider business context. Some companies used the objective input and experience of an outside consultant, but most combined what they described as "a common-sense approach" with help from the computer manufacturer. The manufacturers never followed a policy of selling computers where they were positively not required and, in our experience, sought with integrity to provide a fair analysis. Their motivation was, however—and still is—a clearly commercial one: to sell or lease a computer wherever it is at all feasible.

Another common failing at this stage was to restrict the analysis, albeit unconsciously, to "how can the computer solve our information problems," instead of asking if they were valid problems.

> ▶ One retail business spent a lot of effort in seeing how the computer could reduce the costs of a complicated stock control system. In fact the correct solution was to simplify the procedures radically. The volume of repetitive administrative work which remained was so small that a computer was obviously uneconomic.

Many studies were conceived in another way. They became preoccupied with questions of *technical* feasibility—the volume and collection of data, processing and storage, retrieval methods, appropriate equipment, and support services. While these were obviously important, there were other aspects which could have influenced success or failure. What would be the changes as seen by customers and would they be favorably or unfavorably received? Was it certain that, even if it were technically possible to solve this information problem, there were not other information problems which could, if solved, have contributed more to profitability? Since the computer is moronic, it requires unequivocal rules to follow . . . just how clear were those rules? Was there any evidence that a system like the one being considered was working satisfactorily elsewhere? What problems would arise in securing the wholehearted understanding and commitment of the staff? How would the new information system integrate with existing patterns of formal and informal information? What were the organizational implications of introducing a new computer-based system? In other words, top management should have explored critically and sensitively the operational and human feasibility, as well as the technical realities. Even the most experienced computer experts ran into problems when considering the economic justification for the installation. For example, it was possible to quantify savings in financial charges resulting from tighter automatic credit control, but how did one evaluate the loss of goodwill if good customers were overpressed to settle by a "standard letter" routine? How could one evaluate the hidden benefits which arose when managers, released from some routine drudgery or equipped with new information patterns, were stimulated to think about new business opportunities? Companies installed computers to improve financial results and, as the classic *McKinsey 1968 Report*[3] said:

There are just three ways such results can be reflected in the income statement, and three general categories of computer applications by which this can be accomplished directly:

| | Purpose | Applications |
|---|---|---|
| 1. | To reduce general and administrative expenses | Administrative and accounting uses |
| 2. | To reduce cost of goods sold | Operations control systems |
| 3. | To increase revenues | Product innovation and improved customer service |
| | Improved financial results, of course, can also be achieved indirectly, through better management information and control. This gives rise to a final purpose and application category: | |
| 4. | To improve staff work and management decisions | Information systems and simulation models |

**Figure 1.2**

It seemed comparatively easy to produce a sound economic case in the first category, and this was where most computer applications historically took place. However, the repetition of existing accounting and administrative systems on a computer was rarely found to be economic. Had management thought strategically about the effective computer, certainly more installations would have been made in the last three categories.

## Stage 2. Overdelegation by top management

In the belief that the next stage should be done by experts, the board and senior management recruited (from outside and inside the business) and trained systems analysts and programmers—i.e., people who understood computers—and delegated to them the job of installing the computer. Since these experts were probably the only people in the organization who understood what the computer could do, and were also usually the only ones who were highly motivated to get the system working, the job of deciding the detail of what was to be done was virtually left to them. It is true that the best systems analysts allowed some time for the task of "getting user's agreement," but in projects involving several man-years' work this rarely amounted to real participation.

This overdelegation stemmed from a number of causes. As indicated in stage 1, top management was insecure and uninformed about the technicalities of the computer, and it was only human nature to anticipate that their involvement would be less than in areas with which they were familiar. The barrage of jargon—"peripherals," "bytes," "random access," and so on—put up by the specialists only encouraged this insecurity. In any case, top management often believed that once the decision had been made, implementation could be delegated. Unfortunately, the definition of end results from the computer, the clarity of the plan for implementation, the precise control needed to check time, quality and costs, and the wider implications for the overall business were usually not clear at the feasibility stage. The computer men who were implementing had to use their judgment in interpreting management's needs. Our studies show that the conventional steering committee usually proved to be an imperfect device for guidance and control.

This problem of overdelegation and inadequate involvement is becoming much more serious today, as computer systems impinge on major operational and management matters. In the early and mid 'sixties, some 80 percent of computer time was taken up by processing traditional accounting information. The accountant usually controlled the computer, and he and his systems experts could get along with minimum involvement by others.

### Stage 3. Confusion of objectives

Overdelegation to specialists led to:

SEPARATISM. The computer men talked of line managers as "backwoodsmen." The managers talked of computer men as "longhaired guys who don't understand operational reality."

FEAR. "The computer will take away many jobs." "The computer will expose our failings."

IGNORANCE. Line managers did not know enough about the computer to use it properly.

> ► The warehouse manager in a major confectionery business was struggling with inventory management and recruited extra clerks. He was aware that a computer existed, but thought it was "something they got for the accountants." He had no idea that it could help him with his problems.

PROFESSIONAL SELF-INDULGENCE. The computer specialists often became frustrated by the slow pace at which the project was moving and management's inability to be precise about policies, assumptions, rules, and so on. Increasingly, the danger arose that they would become motivated by the challenge of technical and professional problems, rather than business and operational problems.

> ► In one corporation the computer manager put forward the proposal that each of the senior managers should have a desk terminal in his office. They could then interrogate the computer on a wide range of subjects and get up to date information. The president was shocked at the huge cost and technical complexity of this proposal. He did not deny the value of some limited real-time applications for certain middle managers handling logistical problems. But he believed that a comprehensive system for top management would be expensive and give virtually no help in the kind of strategic decisions they actually faced. He accused the computer manager of "professional self-indulgence" at the company's expense.

The objectives for the computer project became thoroughly confused. The original objectives, still held by the board and senior management, were seen to be misconceived. No analysis of business needs was made at the beginning, and later it was seen to be untrue that the computer reduced staff levels and costs. There was usually a serious lack of user objectives, since middle management did not yet know what they could realistically expect from the machine. On the other hand, there were strong technical objectives held by the computer experts, who sought to automate control procedures on a large scale.

## Stage 4. Cost escalation

Invariably, at this stage, costs escalated—sometimes dramatically—beyond the original estimates. It was only after the project was well under way that the technical problems involved in carrying out the original proposal were fully appreciated. The time required to fulfill original promises lengthened. Top management felt trapped. It was too deeply committed—financially and otherwise—to retreat. Its experts advised a bigger machine, more programmers, etc. At this stage, they could only accede to these requests, or cut back on the scope of the project.

If cost escalation was a problem at this stage in a first application, we found that it usually became even more acute after several years of using the computer. The classic pattern of "what went wrong" shows that the original investment in a computer could be just the tip of the iceberg.

A study of more than 200 firms carried out by Urwick Dynamics showed that over 90 per cent put forward a proposal for replacing or increasing the size of the original computer within three years of the machine being installed. The reasons varied from "our computer is not big enough to cope with the job it has to do" to "our present machine has become obsolete."

Whatever the specific reason, in general these increases amounted in many cases to more than double the first investment. Furthermore, it seems that this cost "escalation" continued in about three-year cycles. Figure 1.3 shows a typical computer investment history.

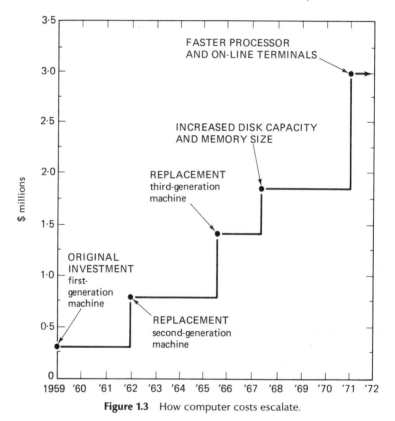

**Figure 1.3**   How computer costs escalate.

In this actual case, there was a total investment of around $3 million on computers, spread over 12 years. During this time, five decisions (at about 2½-yearly intervals) were made to increase the investment, each decision involving $600,000 on average. This history cannot be dismissed as applying only to the early "pioneering" days for computers.

At first sight, we might think that proposals for increasing the investment in computers should present no special problems. The board should be able to measure what it had got for its money from its first machine—or should understand the costs and benefits involved, and be able to consider the proposal like any other plan for new plant, further accommodation, or increased business activity. This is not so. After 15 years of "computerization," most firms still feel trapped when they have to consider proposals for investing more in computers.

Let us consider the dilemma facing management boards who, each year, are faced with spending more money on computers. They may be in a worse position to make a decision than they were when they authorized the purchase of their first machines. First, a knowledgeable group *within* their own firm will put forward strong technical reasons to invest more. The rest of the firm, who might or might not benefit from the investment, may still not have sufficient knowledge to challenge these reasons. Secondly, the firm will now be firmly committed to computer processing. Certain jobs will have been automated and the cost of going back to manual processing would be considerable. On the other hand, the board will be aware of the users' disappointment with the results achieved so far.

Typical of the reasons put forward by computer departments for more equipment are the following:

> There's a lot more to this job than anyone thought four years ago. For one thing, the file sizes have turned out to be three times the volume estimated in the original proposal. And as for saying it would need 12 computer programs—well, we've already written 42 and still the job is only half finished.

. . . which is to say, the manufacturers or the original justification study team (now left?) underestimated the size of the job!

> You don't save money by just doing order processing on the machine. The real payoff is the extra information that computers can give management about our customers, the market, deliveries, stock positions, and so on. But we can't provide this information at the moment—if you want to get the big benefits, we've got to have a big machine.

. . . which is to say, there is a need to do extra jobs on the computer!

> The manufacturers said it would process an order on average in 1.2 seconds. But we can't get the single item orders through in less than 4 seconds average, let alone the multis. Well, the master file takes 4 ¼ hours to process, which just makes nonsense of that 30,000 characters per second claim. . . . And then how did they think 16,000 words of core store would be enough? The software in this machine takes up 12,000 words before we start. . . .

. . . which is to say, the manufacturers oversold their equipment!

Faced with these arguments for further equipment, it can be salutary to ask the following questions:

1.  Who says so? Is it the computer users in the company, the profit centers, the people who stand to get the benefits from this investment? Or is it the computer department, a cost center, which is putting forward these proposals on its own?
2.  What benefits are being put forward to justify this further investment? Are they *measured* business improvements which could not otherwise be achieved? What *measured* business improvements were achieved as a result of the first investment?

Above all, the board should not allow itself to think that there is really no practical alternative to the proposals put to it.

> In one case, we found that the originally envisaged order processing job could not be done on the existing computer because it called for "open item" accounts to be held on the computer file. No measurable business benefit could be discovered from adopting this strategy. On the contrary, by adopting a "balance only" automated system and allowing human beings to hold the account details and deal with queries, a reduction in debtors outstanding from 3.7 to 2.9 months was achieved, releasing $840,000 of capital (the cost of the computer installation). The extra equipment proposed, costing $120,000, was shown to be completely unnecessary.

But this is only one of the alternatives that can be investigated. Computer users should insist on identifying a business benefit from the proposal, just as they should have done for the initial computer installation. The user's commitment to the new proposal must be carefully assessed, since in the end it is the user who will secure the benefit. Even if a benefit can be demonstrated, there may be cheaper equipment, a more efficient installation, or indeed, the use of outside computer services to consider.

We have found that these classic four stages strike a chord with the great majority of computer users. And whenever this classic and depressing sequence is found, it is hardly surprising that surveys reveal that top management is disappointed with the computer.

## Five fundamental misconceptions

Underlying many of the difficulties we have described is a series of fundamental misconceptions about the computer:

## 1. The computer is a mysterious black box for doing large and complex computations

The historical origin of the computer was as a tool for the mathematician. Although it does this job well, the present scale of business investment in the computer cannot be justified for this purpose alone. The computer in business is best thought about as an *information machine* which takes in *raw data* (facts and figures) and *converts* them (by interpreting, classifying, comparing, sorting) into *information* of value to a *user*—i.e., it is relevant, timely, accurate enough, easy to understand, consistent, and manageable. A helpful analogy is to view information, like electricity, as energy. Just as electrical energy is energy which helps us to perform mechanical tasks, so information provides "energy" for decision making and control.

As for the "mysterious box" misconception, it is no more necessary for the average manager to understand the theory and technical detail of the computer than it is for him to understand the theory of electrical generation before he switches on a light. A sensible grasp of the essential features and terminology of computer systems is all that is required. A brief description of basic facts about the computer, prepared by the National Computing Centre Ltd, is included as Appendix 1.

## 2. The computer's main job is to replace human beings

Unless we can find a human being who is behaving completely as an automaton, we cannot replace him with a machine. The computer is essentially complementary to man, not a replacement for him. Some things it can handle very well: as, for example, when parts of the control procedures in an organization have evolved to the point at which they are a reflex, rule-following reaction. The important contribution is not that this necessarily *replaces* men (though sometimes it can, where, say, an army of clerks is doing reflex, rule-following work), but that it *releases* them to undertake the more important discretionary control. This important theme will be developed further in Part 2—"The Effective Computer."

## 3. The computer is a ready to use machine

A surprising number of people behave as though the computer, rather like the office typewriter, will be useful as soon as it is purchased and installed. Certainly, this naive misconception leads to constant frustration and disappointment when analysis, programming, trial runs, and technical complications all cause delay before anything really useful happens. As Isaac Auerbach, president of the Auerbach Corporation, said, "Almost all other machinès were invented to do something when switched on. Unless a computer has been instructed what to do through its program, the only thing it does when switched on is to make a little heat and very little light."

## 4. The economic justification for the computer is cost displacement

This may have been a major consideration when simple applications, such as payroll and accounting systems, dominated the computer's work. It is now much too narrow a view. As we said earlier, the computer's growing role is to open up entirely new opportunities for profitability, not just to reduce the clerical work force. In Peter Drucker's words, "The kindergarten stage is over."

## 5. The computer system and management information systems are synonymous

This misconception has probably been built up by persuasive articles and "sales promotions" in which the manager is depicted as knowing everything about everything as soon as it happens! A typical statement is:

> The goal of . . . the "total systems concept" . . . is nothing less than the complete monitoring of the business enterprise by a computer . . .; the automatic control by the machine of inventories, production scheduling, shipments, accounting, payrolls, and all other operations that can be reduced to mathematical representation; and the limiting of direct human control to such functions as setting overall objectives and reacting to such totally unexpected situations as earthquakes or wars.

Right now, and in the foreseeable future, the computer's contribution to management information is going to be much less "total" and comprehensive. Even some of the routine, reflex controls will always be uneconomical to computerize. Furthermore, there are many vital areas in the management information system which cannot be quantified or, as yet, measured: the morale and commitment of a work force; an entrepreneurial judgment about a new service for customers; a strategic assessment of political developments in a major export market. The computer's contribution is great enough in its own right without exaggerating it to the absurdity of being able to supply all information needed to make any decision.

Our colleague, John Green, has defined management information systems (MIS) thus:

> It is the task of managers to make decisions on the effective provision and allocation of resources to meet the objectives of a business. To make these decisions, managers need information concerning the internal activities of the firm and its external environment. It is the function of a management information system to contribute toward these needs.

Figure 1.4 makes it clear that the computer-based system can be just *one* of a number of information inputs, not the only input. It is also useful to remember that information systems existed long before the computer was invented!

Perspective can be gained by examining major technological breakthroughs in man's history. The *wheel* was a revolutionary invention which opened up entirely new ways to solve our *transportation* problems. It has not (yet) made legs, boats, and other transportation tools obsolete. *Electricity*, although it revolutionized the "energy" business, is, of course, not the only source of useful energy. So with the *computer*! It is a dramatic and fundamental new capability for managing *information*, and one which we are only beginning to comprehend and use wisely. But many other tools of information processing and communication are also important and will not be superseded by computers.

| Phase | Type of decision | Information required | Planning versus control | Time scale | Performance measurement | Manager responsible |
|---|---|---|---|---|---|---|
| Strategic planning | Highly unstructured. No constraints. | Environmental. Unpredictable. Often unquantified. | Planning dominant. | Leisurely decision cycle. Perhaps 5–10 years. | Difficult to measure because of long time scale. | Board and top managers. |
| Tactical planning (and control) | Familiar types of decisions. Wide, clearly defined constraints. | Highly abstracted. Internal. Sometimes predictable. | Planning and control. | Generally 1–5 years. | Measurable after careful analysis. | Top and middle managers. |
| Operational | Highly structured, repetitive decisions. Narrow constraints. | Detailed and clearly defined. | Control dominant. | Monthly, weekly, even daily. | Well established against standards. | Middle or junior managers. |

**Figure 1.4** Phases of management process and their decision types. (A condensed version of a diagram by John Green, Urwick Orr and Partners Limited.)

## References

1. *Computers in Business* National Computing Centre Ltd, p. 12.
2. A list of some recent surveys is included in the bibliography to this book.
3. *Unlocking the Computer's Profit Potential. A Research Report to Management* McKinsey and Co, 1968.

# Part 2
# The effective computer

# Introduction

That there are some disappointments with computers is hardly surprising since we are still in the process of "learning together" how to get the best out of them. Fifteen years or so is a very short time in which to analyze, comprehend, and solve the complex new technical, organizational, and human problems which have arisen. Against these disappointments one can already find many successful installations. Analyzing the benefits arising in such installations, we have found that they fall into one or more of the following groups:

Improving performance of existing rule-following tasks.

Facilitating the increase in volume of existing rule-following tasks where more human beings, for one reason or another, cannot be recruited to do them.

Freeing human beings from existing rule-following tasks to concentrate on goal-seeking, judgment tasks.

Improving performance in an important decision-making area by replacing part of the judgment involved by some rule-following data processing.

Before examining and illustrating these benefits it must be repeated that we can only succeed if two things are understood:

**1. The computer department is a service department.** The computer only provides a service to those who produce and sell the company's products. Benefits, in any organization, can in essence be broken down into two types. Either we obtain more for the things we offer (sell more or sell the same at a higher price) or we spend less in making and selling them. Those who run the computer do not usually have the responsibility for selling, pricing, or production efficiency. It is not open to them to obtain benefits directly. Their role, therefore, must be to help those who *can* achieve benefits.

This may seem so obvious as to be hardly worth stating again. It seems, however, that while most people accept this statement in principle, the failure to follow it through in practice is overwhelmingly the single biggest cause of computer disappointment, and the observance of the principle the major reason for successful installations. The whole of the effective computer approach which we describe is, therefore, designed with this basic idea in mind—it is an approach *to enable users to get business improvements.*

Three further points are worth noting here. Firstly, a large number of computers are used in non–profit-making environments. The principle outlined above applies in exactly the same way in such cases, but the "business improvements" must, of course, be translated from profit into the appropriate objectives of that organization, whatever these may be. Secondly, computer time itself may be the thing a particular business sells. In this case, of course, the computer department can directly influence business performance. It can sell more time; it can provide it more cheaply. This is the special case of the computer service bureau, and, while not relevant to our general discussion, it serves as a further illustration of the basic point. Unless computer services are sold to paying customers outside the organization, as distinct from internal users of the service, the computer cannot directly influence profit. Thirdly, computer department cost reduction is an exception to what we have been saying. If computer costs are cut without affecting the services provided, business profits will rise. This is important. We devote the whole of Part 3 to improving the efficiency of computer departments. But it has limited potential: the main concern of this book is to exploit the potential of the computer. Important though cost reduction is, let us concentrate in this part on improving effectiveness rather than efficiency.

**2. The contribution and nature of the computer must be understood.** The classic "failure sequence" and fundamental misconceptions already described reflect, above all, a widespread ignorance about the nature and contribution of computers. Without understanding and adequate knowledge it is inevitable that insecurity, antagonism, and well-intentioned incompetence in computer usage will result. We return to this theme in a

| Human being | Computer |
|---|---|
| Can see overall problems and relationships: perceives specific problems in context of an environment or experience not itself quantified completely. | Can be programmed to deal with complex issues, e.g., a moon landing, but only where the action required can be predicted by man. Computer will continue to obey rules when they cease to be relevant. Strength is in handling repetitive operations where quantified rules can be set, where high speed is desirable, and where man continually monitors the rules' relevance. |
| Can learn from experience, draw on imagination, creative powers, judgment, and common sense. | Can only do what the hardware/software designers tell it to do. |
| Not always accurate, and behavior not fully predictable. | Consistent. |
| Flexible, can handle the unexpected. | Inflexible in the sense that it can only handle the "unexpected" if it has been programmed beforehand to do so for the specific event. Some small "learning ability" can be designed, but it often proves more economical to refer the unexpected at once to a human being. |
| Capacious memory but not very precise "retrieval." Rather forgetful. | Smaller memory in range but can be comprehensive in selected areas (e.g., account and balance for *all* customers). Very precise and speedy retrieval. Never forgets. |
| Relatively slow in handling complex quantified data. | Relatively fast in handling complex quantified data. |
| A rich and subtle language for interpersonal communication and thought. | Unambiguous language limited to commanding the computer's small range of actions. |

**Figure 2.1**

later section on training and managing change, but it is already clear that this understanding will not be easy to acquire. It is certainly not just a question of enrolling managers in computer courses to teach them how the machine works, or of enrolling computer specialists in business courses to teach them management. Before we develop our effective computer approach of contributing toward users' achievements, let us see, first, if our computer experience so far will help us to gain some understanding of what this contribution might be.

## Successful computers: a common pattern

If, by and large, computers have not paid their way by saving staff, what have they achieved? The cases that demonstrate effective use of computers, and where management and computer staff are satisfied with their investment, all have one thing in common:

> The company is achieving something, with the aid of its computer, that it would not have achieved without it.

When we analyze these cases, the nature of the computer's contribution seems to lie in one or more of the following four areas.

### 1. Improved performance of repetitive tasks

The point to stress in this area (and in the other three areas described below) is that the abilities of humans and computers are complementary. In no sense is the computer a replacement for a human being as far as control is concerned. It performs control in an entirely different way. Sometimes the human approach is better, sometimes that of the computer (see Figure 2.1). The difference between the two methods is illustrated in Figure 2.2.

| Machine | Man |
|---|---|
| Rule-following | Goal-seeking |
| Obedient | Willful |

**Figure 2.2**

We have said that computers are rule-following. In performing any computation, in providing any item of information, the computer first has to have the rules described to it (in a computer program) for carrying out this work. It follows that once these rules are given to it the computer is completely obedient. It will carry them out consistently (accurately, tirelessly, without challenge) forever after, barring mechanical failure.

Man, on the other hand, is not rule-following. He can be taught rules, but unless he can so absorb them that they become a subconscious habit, he is very bad at carrying them out. Conscious rule-following bores him. He tires, he is inconsistent, inaccurate, forgetful, and frequently prefers his own view of the matter to the rules he has been given. His genius lies in achieving goals when the rules for getting there are not known. In novel situations, he is able to work out for himself what to do. By the same token, however, he is willful rather than obedient. He "wants" things—he is not indifferent to the goals. He chooses his path toward them; he is not blindly directed.

If we find some large-scale clerical task which is essentially repetitive, therefore, it is almost certain that we shall improve its performance (accuracy, consistency, etc.) if we give it to a computer.

▶ A firm in the chemicals industry sold its products in expensive containers. Its policy was to charge for these containers, and refund the money when the container was returned. The vast number of containers involved, the casual nature of their return, and the problems of reuse strained the clerical system for recording where they were.

Inaccuracies in the records caused endless disputes with customers and delayed payment of invoices. The computer brought an accuracy to the control system which clerks could not achieve. The firm was able to make substantial inroads into the outstanding queries on containers, and thereby reduce the accounts receivable by more than $1,200,000.

▶ The rules for debt collection in a public utility company were clearly laid down. They were not followed consistently by the clerks, who allowed amounts to accumulate beyond the credit limits. Furthermore, the pressure of ongoing bookkeeping work prevented them from vigorously tightening up the rules for persistently bad payers. The consistent application of the rules by the computer enabled the firm to bring the average age of accounts receivable down by 2.2 weeks. The sums involved were so large that this saving alone paid for the computer system.

## 2. Increased volume of repetitive tasks

Humans with the ability and education needed to do certain repetitive work are no longer prepared to do it. How often do we hear the shortage-of-staff cry? But we are not short of qualified people—there are more now than there ever were. They simply will not do repetitive, boring tasks. And when clerks do perform repetitive work the lack of job satisfaction drives them, like industrial workers, to join unions in order to increase their salary compensation for the work.

Here, we see another force at work encouraging the beneficial use of computers for repetitive tasks. Slowly, but very surely, we are seeing clerks price themselves out of this work, which is unsuitable for human beings in any case.

We find beneficial computer applications, therefore, where corporate objectives cannot be achieved for want of clerical labor.

> ▶ A building and loan association had the market opportunity to increase its volume of business. They recognized that the main constraint restricting their expansion was "shortage of staff." They found they were unable to attract into clerical work people with the ability, accuracy, careful attitude, and sense of responsibility that the job demanded. Such people had received good education and were able to get jobs offering more satisfaction, opportunities, and salary. A computer-based control system reduced their recruitment problem and enabled the association to cope with the increased volume of data, and thus to achieve their objectives.

### 3. Humans released for discretionary tasks

Where the benefits from computer processing of rule-following tasks are not significant, cases arise in which it is still worth implementing computer processing, for the following reason. Humans may in this way gain the opportunity to improve their achievements in the discretionary (goal-seeking) area because a computer system has relieved them of the burden of having to carry out the rule-following system. This further exploits our idea of complementary abilities set out earlier—by enabling humans to concentrate on the area in which they perform better.

> ▶ An ocean liner corporation lost many hundreds of thousands of dollars over a period of years because of errors in notifying passenger reservations, and delays in notifying subsequent changes, by local travel agents, who acted independently and were not under the corporation's control. The corporation's accountants could not concentrate on these reservation queries since they were fully occupied doing the routine bookkeeping. A computer system was introduced to handle ongoing bookkeeping. The accountants concentrated on the queries, work which involved human judgment since each case was different. Within one year, the outstanding queries carried over from each voyage disappeared.

> ▶ A bookmaker could not retain his trained staff through the winter (the slack racing season). When the volume of betting rose each summer he could not recruit and train enough staff to cope. He computerized his routine

accounts. He coped easily with the volume of summer betting. His staff was free to concentrate on the goal of increasing their sales. Eighteen months later, he introduced an entirely new type of bet, which caught on and increased revenue by 60 per cent. Previously no one in the firm had been able to think about how to increase the volume of work because the critical preoccupation was coping with the routine accounting for the volume of bets they already had.

## 4. Improved control method

The last category of benefit embraces cases in which a decision, previously made entirely by human judgment, can be improved with the help of some rule-following data processing. This benefit involves a basic change in the method of making the decision, from "seat of the pants" to "scientific" management. The nature of the improvements in these cases is not so much that people fail to realize that a rule-following or logical approach to taking the decision would have been better; it is rather that the rules to be followed are too complicated or the volume of data to be processed too great to make it a practical possibility for human beings to do. This benefit covers such cases as sale managers who base their selling strategy on their judgment of how their market is responding, because getting the actual information from the sales accounts would be too laborious for clerks, too slow, and too inaccurate. It covers cases of production managers who use experience and judgment to make marginal adjustments to planning schedules, because examining all the alternatives would be impracticable and error prone.

▶ The managing director of a chain of retail grocery stores knew that the information which would improve his sales and stocking policy actually existed in the stores order records. "But I dare not ask for it," he said. "The trouble is they would try and get it. They would come in weekends, slave over the figures, and give me a wrong answer two weeks later. And if I said 'that's interesting, what would happen if we excluded Crawley and Maidenhead' there's a danger they'd have a go at that one, too!"

▶ A shipping firm, engaged in shipping freight in containers (each costing $1,200 or more) sought to improve the efficiency of its container utilization. The human control system relied on local agents requisitioning the number of containers they needed. This "judgment" method of allocating stocks encouraged a built-in buffering system, since each agent tended to ask for more containers than he really needed on the off-chance that another shipment order might come in. A computer container allocation system based on rules taking account of orders actually received, the available stocks, and the probabilities of future orders, reduced the number of containers required to handle the same volume of goods by 4 per cent, resulting in a saving of $3,000,000 per annum.

We can summarize by restating that an analysis of successful computer installations shows that benefits can be achieved in one or more of four ways.

Improving performance of existing rule-following tasks.

Facilitating the increase in volume of existing rule-following tasks when more human beings, for one reason or another, cannot be recruited to do them.

Freeing human beings from existing rule-following tasks to concentrate on goal-seeking, judgment tasks.

Improving performance in an important decision-making area by replacing part of the judgment involved by some rule-following data processing.

Note that in none of the cases mentioned above is the computer success achieved through staff savings. In each case, the computer enables the user to achieve some previously defined benefit, e.g., to reduce debtors, increase market share, or reduce container costs.

## 5. Setting business improvement objectives for computers

We have just identified two entirely different areas of control. Let us call the rule-following area *reflex control* from now on, and the goal-seeking area *discretionary control*. We have suggested that the computer's contribution to business will come from its application to reflex control. Such reflex control will improve, since computers are better at this than humans, and also the computer will release human beings to concentrate on their great strength, discretionary control.

Armed with this insight into the nature of the computer's contribution, let us turn to the first problem we identified in making computers effective. Namely, computers are a service department. Computer departments cannot themselves get business benefits. We said, therefore, that our approach must be essentially to get the computer to help those who can get benefits, i.e., the users of the computer systems. Once we try to do this, we come across three difficulties, all well known to data processing managers, but nevertheless so important that they are worth stressing again:

**(a) How do we identify the right user benefits to go for?** So many computer installations have become a disappointment to senior management

—not because the computer projects have been in any way badly handled, but because the wrong objectives were set in the first place. For example, in almost all cases studied in which the objective was to obtain clerical savings, it was found that this was the wrong benefit at which to aim.

**(b) How do we identify the computer's contribution toward the achievement of this benefit?** Given a proper objective, e.g., the expansion of the business by 40 per cent in the do-it-yourself market, what role should the computer play?

**(c) How do we actually achieve the benefit?** The point here is that computer systems in themselves achieve nothing.

> ► An automobile components firm set a proper objective to reduce inventory levels by a certain amount, and the role of the computer was correctly identified as providing a reflex control system suggesting reordering quantities based on rules concerning forecasts of future demand, levels of service, and the lead time for replenishment. The system was programmed and implemented, and it worked successfully according to the system specifications. No benefits resulted. On a subsequent audit by consultants, it was found that the objectives for getting the computer system implemented were impeccably defined, allocated, and achieved. No one in the company had the objective of actually reducing the inventory level, however.

Data processing departments, aware that the users must be involved if these difficulties are to be overcome, try many methods to obtain such user involvement, some more successful than others. Occasionally, it is hoped that the difficulties will be solved entirely by the user himself if he is "charged" for computer services using some interdepartmental cross-charging system. The idea, of course, is that if the user has to pay for computer services he is certain to make beneficial use of them. Unfortunately, the user realizes he does not usually know enough about computers to identify their beneficial contribution without the assistance of the computer department. Experience shows that he normally reacts defensively in this situation. Upon being charged for computer services, he challenges the cost of the computer department, sows seeds of doubt concerning its efficiency, and sometimes even succeeds in having its performance "audited"!

These three difficulties really bring us to the heart of the problem—how to get computer experts and computer users together in a constructive attempt to make effective use of computers. The approach which follows was designed as a way to achieve just this, and has proved successful in practice.

## The effective computer: a six-stage approach

The effective computer approach, based on the principles of management by objectives, involves six stages, and is illustrated in Figure 2.3.

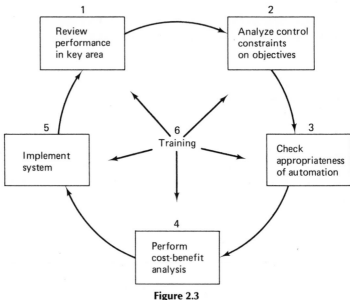

**Figure 2.3**

In summary, the first step is to identify the key areas of the business. Our intention is to secure a worthwhile benefit from automation. Computer systems commonly cost hundreds of thousands of dollars, and we shall be wasting our time if we concentrate on areas which do not offer high potential for improvement. The key areas of a business (in Management by Objectives terms) are those few activities in which good or bad performance has a major effect on profit.

Having identified a particular key area in which performance is vital (e.g., cash flow in a company short of funds; volume of sales in an excess-capacity company trading around the breakeven point), we next set objectives for improved performance in this key area, and see whether the present control system will prevent us from achieving them. If so, would it be possible to achieve the objectives with a computer system, bearing in mind the four ways in which computers can make a contribution?

If we have a major business benefit which cannot, as a practical measure, be achieved without a computer system, then we have identified an area for automation. Note that this approach differs from those which simply attempt to perform some existing system better (cheaper, faster, more accurately, etc.). In our approach, the computer system is seen from the start as an aid to achieving some *new* business objective. The area of interest is next examined (stage 3 in Figure 2.3) to see if it is entirely suitable for automation. Will it create other unacceptable jobs, will it adversely affect our customers, can rules be designed which really do cover the situation, etc.?

Once this test is passed, stage 4 is to carry out a cost–benefit analysis for the proposed applications. Again, this analysis differs from those which seek to offset the computer system's costs with the savings to be achieved. In this case, the benefit is the measured value of the new business objective to be achieved.

Stage 5 consists of the implementation of the computer project.

Stage 6 covers training, which, though mentioned last, is in fact taking place throughout the approach. The previous five stages will all have been performed by mixed teams of users and computer specialists. During this work, training in how computers may contribute to business results takes place in a more valuable way for all those participating than can be provided in any formal training course alone.

Let us go through each of these six stages in detail to see how they are undertaken.

### Stage 1. Key areas analysis

In this stage, we are trying to identify the really important activities of the company. In any organization, if we analyze all the work areas, we can usually find five or six which are crucial to the organization's success. We

**Figure 2.4**

are here following one of Peter Drucker's main principles—the principle of concentration. If we are seeking to make a business improvement, let us concentrate our attempts in the few areas that really influence profits.

An analysis of key areas in a business is not easy—it takes a lot of self-critical thinking—but it is a most valuable preliminary discipline to the design of any information system, computer based or not, which is to make an effective contribution. In this way, we shall be applying our efforts where they count most.

The key areas will, of course, vary from time to time as different problems face the firm and different opportunities arise. Typically, the analyst asks three searching questions:[1]

(a)  What is our purpose? That is, what are we in business for? What are the needs of our customers that we are trying to satisfy? What major changes do we want to bring about in the firm during the next three to five years (markets, profits, operating methods, etc.)?
(b)  What is the present situation of our firm? That is, what are the strengths and weaknesses of our firm at the moment (internal analysis)? What are the opportunities and what are the threats that face us (external analysis)?[1]
(c)  Given our present situation, what are the few (commonly five or six) vital areas of activity which will enable us to fulfill our purpose?

▶ Some years ago, a major airline corporation recognized the opportunity to increase its volume of business, as the total demand for air travel was increasing. Its major strengths were its present dominant position and facilities which would make it easy to take advantage of the increasing demand. A weakness in this connection was its inability to cope efficiently with reservations for the present level of business. Two further threats were identified: the difficulty of getting reservation clerks, and the difficulty of raising further finances to increase the number of aircraft and expand the maintenance facilities to handle the increased volume of business. They identified these three key areas, among others:

   Passenger reservations
   Aircraft scheduling
   Aircraft maintenance

▶ A television corporation identified its purpose as the provision of education, information, and entertainment for the public. Opportunities were many— the popularity of the medium, color, possibility for exploitation of the medium, etc. One of its weaknesses was its inability, both physically and financially, to provide increased production resources to enable improved standards of quality and variety to be achieved in its programs. Among a number of key areas were:

   Program budgeting, i.e., the detailed estimation and approval of the cost of each television program.
   Resource scheduling, i.e., the apportioning of the various available resources, such as studios, camera teams, etc., among the television programs that needed them at various times.

### Stage 2. Analyze the control constraints on objectives

What we are trying to do, in this second stage of our analysis, is to find out how the computer can contribute to the achievements of the line departments in the business, i.e., the makers and the sellers. Essentially, our approach is to identify some major objectives for a line department in one of the key areas—which cannot, as a practical and economic possibility, be achieved without the help of a computer system.

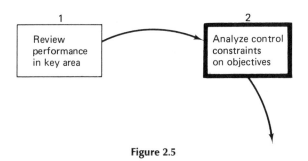

**Figure 2.5**

Clearly, if we can identify such a contribution from automation, then the computer is placed in the forefront of the business. It no longer has the negative role of trying to reduce the overhead—which is regarded, anyway, as an unfortunate burden the company has to carry. It has the positive role of contributing toward a business improvement. This idea of a "strategic role" for computers emerged clearly at a recent interview with a man applying for a senior systems analyst post with an airline corporation. The candidate was an ambitious young man, and was asked why he wished to leave his present job. "Computers are my career," he said. "But in my company nobody understands what they can do. We don't feel part of the firm. I want to join an organization where the computer is in the front line of the business."

While agreeing with the idea of a strategic role for computers, some people take the view that it is only rarely possible to achieve such a role and that airlines, missile control, banking, etc., are isolated examples of activities which just happen to have potential computer applications which affect the heart of their operations.

This is not true! The scope for automation will vary from activity to activity and in some cases the strategic role for the computer will be more obvious than in others. But only the understanding and attitude of the corporation's personnel determines the function of their computer, and the kind of benefit they can produce from it.

People get together in organizations because together they can do things which they cannot do on their own. But coordinating the actions of a number of people creates a control problem that a one-man business does not have. And this control difficulty gets worse as the size or complexity of the organization increases. Without exception, every ambitious objective for improving performance brings with it a new control problem. This is the area in which we should search for computer applications, since it is here we shall find their strategic role. Examples of objectives in key areas of companies are shown below.

| | |
|---|---|
| *Corporation:* | Aircraft spares |
| *Key area:* | Market share |
| *Objective:* | To increase sales volume by 40 per cent by . . . |
| *Contributory systems objective for computer:* | To install an on-line CRT display system in customers' premises showing our stock and delivery position and price |

| | |
|---|---|
| *Corporation:* | Soft-drinks manufacturer, bottler, and distributor |
| *Key area:* | Distribution |
| *Objective:* | To reduce distribution costs by $528,000 by . . . . |
| *Contributory systems objective for computer:* | To implement a trucking and warehouse optimization system |

| | |
|---|---|
| *Corporation:* | Cable manufacturer |
| *Key area:* | Price fixing |
| *Objective:* | To improve profitability (on existing sales volume) by $204,000 by . . . . |
| *Contributory systems objective for computer:* | To implement a cable material and labor analysis system showing detailed variable costs and profit contributions of each product |

| | |
|---|---|
| *Corporation:* | Building and construction |
| *Key area:* | Contract bidding |
| *Objective:* | Improve profit margin by 2 per cent on existing turnover |
| *Contributory systems objective for computer:* | Implement profit margin maximization system, suggesting optimum bid based on analysis of previous bidding patterns of competitors |

| | |
|---|---|
| *Corporation:* | Aircraft manufacturer |
| *Key area:* | Market share |
| *Objective:* | To reduce the time for release of any group of new orders to a maximum of 24 hours from the time of receipt |
| *Contributory systems objective for computer:* | To implement a system for calculating production requirements based on the latest design situation, accumulate new and brought-forward production commitments, and release production work orders aligned with the required production program and the requirements of economical batch processing |

| | |
|---|---|
| *Corporation:* | Carton manufacturer |
| *Key area:* | Productivity |
| *Objective:* | To reduce waste on corrugated box manufacture by 8 per cent by . . . . |
| *Contributory systems objective for computer:* | To implement an order analysis system for determining optimum width and run size for corrugated paper |
| | |
| *Corporation:* | An electrical goods manufacturer |
| *Key area:* | Working capital |
| *Objective:* | To reduce work in progress by 10 per cent by . . . . |
| *Contributory systems objective for computer:* | To implement a "bought out" and production control information system showing quantities and dates required for all components every 24 hours, up to date within three hours |
| | |
| *Corporation:* | Television |
| *Key area:* | Advertising revenue |
| *Objective:* | To decrease underutilization of advertising air time by 75 per cent |
| *Contributory systems objective for computer:* | To implement a real-time rescheduling system to obtain improved fit of clients' requirements to available time, and to allow acceptance of later bookings |

Such objectives do not have to be directly linked to increased profitability:

| | |
|---|---|
| *Corporation:* | An engineering company supplying its product to a number of governments |
| *Key area:* | Spare parts provisioning |
| *Objective:* | To reduce the time for agreeing the initial stocks of spare parts for products supplied, from 18 months to six months |
| *Contributory systems objective for computer:* | To implement a system showing the cumulative positions on parts common to more than one section of the product within 12 hours of receiving the decision of each provisioning meeting, thus enabling provisioning meetings to take place at the rate of one per day |

Note two things about these objectives. Firstly, the main objective is held by a line department, the user of the computer system. Only the user can achieve business benefits. The systems objective represents the computer's contribution to the achievement of the main objective. The most important contribution automation can make is to solve control problems that are preventing the achievement of the line department's objective. We have already discussed the four main areas in which this will occur. The second thing to note is that each of the main objectives is quantified. This idea of setting *measured* objectives is fundamental to the idea of MBO. The reason for setting measured objectives is not only to assess and compare peoples' performances. Where this is their main use, MBO soon falls into disrepute and fails. Instead, there are two other, more important reasons. Firstly, there is the discipline of trying to quantify objectives. For example, by saying: "Reduce inventory levels to $1,200,000 by January 1, 1973, maintaining established levels of service," instead of: "Achieve stock reduction," we force such objectives to be considered realistically. Probably, anybody is prepared to be committed to getting an "improvement." But before agreeing to get a specified stock reduction by a specified date the manager must ask questions such as:

Is this target really attainable?

What change must I make in my methods, organization, resources, skills, etc., to achieve it?

What other people are involved? What must they do to enable me to achieve this objective (especially, what control system will I need)?

Most important, the discipline of setting measured targets should encourage the preparation of plans at an appropriate level of detail and the commitment of all who are involved in achieving the contributory objectives.

Secondly, measured objectives facilitate proper reviews. If we just say we will obtain better credit control, it is impossible to assess at any particular time whether we have achieved our objective satisfactorily, or are likely to achieve it.

By way of illustration of stage 2, let us look further at the airline and television corporations considered in stage 1.

▶ The airline corporation set its overall objective as achieving an increase in traffic volume of 60 per cent. Having established its key areas, the corporation set objectives in each of them. Namely,

Passenger reservation: to handle a 60 per cent increase in the volume of bookings

Aircraft scheduling: to achieve a 12 per cent increase in the utilization of aircraft

Aircraft maintenance: to reduce maintenance costs by $1,200,000

It was recognized that the first of these objectives could not be achieved as a practical and economical proposition using human control systems. Each clerk could not hold his own booking records—the overall booking position would have to be available to all reservation clerks. However, the volume of such centralized information could not be stored and looked up in time by human beings. Moreover, information storage and retrieval work is repetitive and, therefore, error prone. Furthermore, humans with the ability to do it are less and less willing to take such a job.

Examination of the second and third objectives revealed that a different method of control in these areas would improve efficiency to the levels required. The problem of optimizing the use of aircraft requires examining the allocation of different aircraft among large numbers of flights. The alternative possibilities were so numerous, and the special conditions (suitability of aircraft, crewing, seasonal variation, etc.) so complex, that humans did not in fact seek an optimum solution. Faced with this sort of problem, the human method of making decisions is to seek a solution which works, and to improve it by making adjustments in the light of experience. Once the rules and the criteria for success are defined, the computer can quickly assess all the possibilities, and thus provide the basis of a new method for making such decisions. This is also the case with aircraft maintenance. The scheduling of maintenance involved too many alternatives for humans to optimize their plans. It was further complicated by the problem of keeping and referring to the records of each aircraft's maintenance history and flying time in order to predict requirements. In all these key areas, therefore, contributory objectives were set for computer control systems:

> to design and implement an on-line passenger reservation system by . . . .

> to design and implement a computer-based flight scheduling planning and optimization system by . . . .

> to store aircraft usage and maintenance records on a computer, and develop a maintenance scheduling information system by . . . .

▶ The television company focused its attention on the key areas of program budgeting and resource scheduling. It set its objectives in resource scheduling as:

> to satisfy producers' increased demands for resources (occasioned by improvements in the variety and quality of programs), and to reduce costs on the outside provision of resources by $240,000 per annum by . . . .

It was decided to achieve this objective by improved planning. A contributory objective was thus set in the key area of program budgeting:

> to produce budgets for each television program six months in advance, so that the need for outside resources would be recognized in time to reschedule requirements.

Humans could not operate such a system satisfactorily. The essential requirement of the system was for producers to see when their plans—considered in conjunction with other producers' plans—caused an overload on resources and, on such occasions, to replan (move programs forward and store them on film until wanted, change requirements, etc.) so as to shift their use from times when a resource was overloaded to times when it was underutilized. There were 60 resources to plan (studios, camera crews, makeup, etc.) and over 300 programs. A computer system was able to work out the implications of producers' "what if" questions during the planning stage sufficiently quickly for them to try alternatives, and thus to achieve the budget objectives. A further contributory objective was set for a computer system, therefore:

> to design and implement a management information system to show the over- and underutilization of resources, given the program plans of each producer, and to produce program budgets resulting from these initial decisions. Also, to produce new resource utilizations and budgets within 24 hours of the notification of revisions to these plans.

The important point about these two cases is that significant measured business improvements were identified which could not be achieved without the help of computer control systems.

## Stage 3. Check appropriateness of automation

Our approach so far has identified potential areas for automation. These areas should not be adopted without making sure that, in helping the

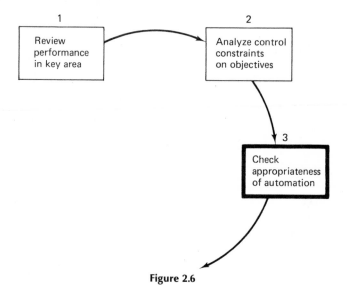

**Figure 2.6**

business to achieve its objectives, automation will not at the same time be the cause of a falling-off of performance in some other field. We have seen that automation is a fundamentally different approach to control from using human beings. A change of this fundamental can upset the balance of the system which already exists. Just as any major change in technology affects the original balance of nature, so automation interferes with the ecology of management within organizations. There are a large number of cases where automated systems—which in themselves represented improvements—caused a worsening in performance overall. An analysis of cases shows seven major and distinct causes of worsening of performance through the introduction of computer systems.

(a) An apparent illogicality, duplication of work, or irrelevancy is, in fact, propping up the system.

> ► A group of four companies, each trading with the same customers, had four separate administration systems. They sought to rationalize their administrative procedures to improve the service they gave to their customers and reduce overhead costs. They introduced a single computer-based system which enabled them to integrate their accounts and achieve their objectives. Accounts receivable increased alarmingly. Previously, customers received a number of separate invoices. Those who had queries delayed payment of only the invoice under query. Under the new system they received a single consolidated invoice. A single query now caused delayed payment of a much larger amount.

(b) A decision based on human judgment or human local knowledge may be preferable to an automated optimized or logical system.

> ► A corporation manufacturing pharmaceuticals had both a home and overseas market. They sought to expand their sales but the service to customers declined as a result, and they achieved little progress. The major problem was the wrong dispatch of orders, items being forgotten or delivered short. The clerical control system could not forecast requirements with sufficient accuracy, and the communication links between order-taking clerks, stock-control clerks, dispatch clerks, and invoicing clerks caused errors and delays. Frequently, items shown in stock when dispatch instructions were made out, were out of stock when people tried to assemble the order. A computer system improved the accuracy, overcame the delays, and thus enabled a reservation system to be operated which ensured that stocks reserved for one order were not dispatched on another. Complaints about wrong dispatches stopped.
>
> They were replaced by worse complaints, however, that delivery times were increasing rapidly. An investigation showed that overseas orders— which normally covered many items—were being held back by the meticulous operation of the rules of the new system, which would not allow the dispatch of an incomplete order. At the same time, all the items which were

in stock for such orders were reserved pending the arrival of the shortages. This caused home-trade orders (usually covering small quantities only) to be held up although stocks were present.

The problem was finally solved by recognizing that, although the automated reservation system was ideal for the home trade, part delivery of overseas orders was preferable, based on the human judgment of what the customer would accept and the local knowledge of the likelihood of supplies arriving quickly.

(c) The automation of work unacceptable to human beings may create similar work in another area.

▶ A company manufacturing a variety of goods in the rubber industry was faced with enormous opportunities for growth in an expanding market. However, they could not get sufficient staff to operate their order processing and invoicing system, and those they did recruit were not able or interested enough to do the job satisfactorily. Furthermore, turnover was very high and they could not cope with the training problems involved with continual recruitment. They automated their order processing system, and successfully removed this particular constraint on their growth.

The company soon found staff problems in two new areas, however. The system demanded a large volume of data on each order to be fed into the computer. They set up a data preparation system which required 80 operators to punch the information onto paper tape. This work was even more uninteresting than the order processing the company had automated, and they failed to recruit and hold a sufficient number of people to do this new task. Furthermore, a number of their sales representatives left the firm soon after the system started, because they complained that nearly half their time was spent in completing computer input documents with details never required before, and with an accuracy and discipline (coding, marking columns, legibility, etc.) which was too burdensome.

(d) Automation may remove a necessary human contact.

▶ A company selling derivatives from detergents had virtually no production function, and concentrated on marketing and distribution. They wished to strengthen their marketing, the key area of their business, with an information system concerning their customers and sales. Their clerks were fully occupied processing orders and invoices—the provision of information was an extra job. The questions asked varied and thus produced sharp peaks. The information to be analyzed was enormous in volume, and the answers were always inaccurate. The company set up a computer-based information system which solved the problem. To provide the information, however, the system first had to process customer orders and issue invoices. This company depended on its personal contact and the special services it gave to its customers. The automated system was rigid in its application of the rules and began to get between the company and its customers. They no longer received the accustomed personal service regarding orders, special deliveries, discounts, accounts queries, etc. The company's representatives no longer had sufficient scope to look after their customers, and sales, instead of being strengthened, suffered a severe setback.

(e) Although rules are laid down, it may be the bending of these rules by human beings that makes the system work.

▶ A corporation quarrying and distributing sand and gravel experienced two major problems in expanding its business. Growth involved acquiring a number of smaller firms, and customer accounts, and order processing needed to be consolidated into a single coordinated system. The corporation had neither the clerks nor the space in their main office to operate a centralized system. Furthermore, they experienced growing inefficiencies in the routing and scheduling of their trucks as the business expanded. They installed a centralized computer system which successfully coordinated their accounts procedure and began to help management improve the utilization of their fleet of trucks.

The system followed the apparently straightforward rule that invoices should include a charge for delivery. A number of customers refused to pay the amounts charged by the computer system, however. Others complained that they had received short delivery. Following the company's efforts to put this right, the utilization of trucks began to fall seriously. On investigation, it was found that the previous manual system had not applied this rule strictly. Deliveries were frequently over or under the amount ordered. But the site control clerks of the regular customers accepted this—they had kept informal local records, shortages being adjusted by subsequent overdeliveries. The insistence by the computer that the amount delivered should always equal the amount ordered removed a flexibility from the system, which had enabled the firm to simplify its accounting and make considerable economies in its delivery system.

(f) The inflexibility of an automated system may hinder the business' adaptation to changing requirements.

▶ A bank wished to increase the number of its customers and to increase the range of services it provided, including credit card facilities. The bulk of its accounting was done locally in its branches, however, and a major constraint in its growth was the difficulty of recruiting and retaining clerks locally to cope with the increasing volume of work. A large computer system was successfully implemented which processed customer accounts centrally and enabled the bank to achieve its objectives. With the removal of much of the accounting work from the branches, however, the local bank manager's role shifted in emphasis, and he became able to concentrate on selling the services of the bank. Recognizing this change in requirements, the systems department analyzed the key decisions made by the bank manager, to see what information should be supplied by the computer system. They found one of the key decisions concerned who should be given loans. This decision depended mainly on an analysis of the interest rates charged to different categories of customers, and for different purposes. This information was not stored in the computer data base, however, since the need for it had not been recognized when the computer system had first been designed. It was found that the customer records could not be adjusted to include this information without rewriting the complete package of programs—which represented some 50 man-years of work.

(g) An automated system may destroy the motivation of the humans who remain involved with it.

▶ An insurance firm introduced a computer system to facilitate the growth of its business without increasing its central office space and staff. This objective was successfully achieved. A new clerical job was created in its offices, however. Previously the clerks had handled the accounts and premiums of their customers personally. They were skilled at their work, interested in it, and derived satisfaction from it. But now the calculations and maintenance of insurance accounts were handled by machine, and the system was standardized to a few alternatives, taking away most of the need to deal with special cases. The clerical job was reduced to making out and checking computer input documents containing the policy and payment data for the computer to process. With the interest taken away from their work, the clerks' morale fell. A number left and were replaced by people with no tradition of interest in the work. The clerks, having monotonous jobs, became "industrial workers." They demanded more pay as compensation and joined unions. Furthermore, the management, who held their position because of their insurance expertise, were completely unable to motivate their staff—they were not trained or experienced in this aspect of management, since the need for it had previously been minimal.

### Stage 4. Perform cost–benefit analysis

In stage 2 we discovered potential areas for automation. In stage 3 we examined them to see if automation might cause more harm than good in the company. Having found candidates surviving this test, in this stage we undertake a cost–benefit analysis. Although figures vary greatly from installation to installation, the following cost–benefit study for a computer system, taken from a mail order company, is typical of the method generally employed:

|  |  |  | $'000s |
|---|---|---|---|
| *Running costs* | Equipment (incl. depreciation) | Computer | 163 |
|  |  | Data preparation | 24 |
|  | Staff | Operators | 38 |
|  |  | Data preparation and control | 58 |
| *Development costs* | Systems |  | 38 |
|  | Programming |  | 53 |
|  | File conversion and maintenance |  | 12 |
|  |  | Total costs | 386 |
| *Tangible benefits* | Clerical savings |  | 221 |
|  | Replacement of conventional equipment |  | 84 |
|  | Space savings |  | 101 |
|  |  | Total tangible benefits | 406 |
|  |  | Savings | 20 |
| *Intangible benefits* | Reduced inventory |  |  |
|  | Improved agent control |  |  |
|  | Improved management information |  |  |

There are a number of interesting points that can be made about such statements. Firstly, the running costs include certain fixed costs, and various accounting methods can be employed to allocate them for project justification. Secondly, development costs are incurred mainly at the beginning, and benefits arrive later; therefore, discounted cash-flow

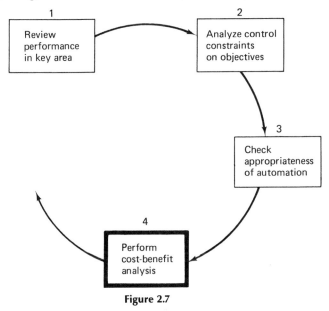

**Figure 2.7**

techniques can be employed in comparing costs and benefits. Thirdly, such statements only measure cost savings benefits, which we have said earlier can never be the sole reason for using computers. Fourthly, strategic benefits are mentioned as merely adding weight (to what is probably only a breakeven case). They are often believed to be un-measurable and classed as "intangible benefits."

It is not part of the effective computer approach to comment on the methods of cost allocation and accounting methods used. The diversity, and the pros and cons of such methods, are now widely known. But it is essential to the effective computer approach that the benefits be assessed differently. Firstly, stage 4 *starts* with the assessment of the benefits—not the costs. Secondly, the benefit is stated as the business objective that was identified and measured in stage 2. Furthermore, costs, using the effective computer approach, are the total costs of achieving the business objective, e.g., the total costs of the plans of all the departments involved in getting the benefit, not just the cost of the computer system. A decision on whether to go ahead is then made on this basis—on a comparison of the business improvement objective with the overall cost of plans to achieve it.

Consider the following example taken from an insurance company:

| Benefit | | $ |
|---|---|---|
| Gross profit improvement from increased business | | 1,068,000 |
| *Increased operating costs* | $ | |
| Additional clerical salaries | 154,000 | |
| Computer service bureau charges | 426,000 | |
| Systems and program maintenance | 79,000 | |
| Premises | 53,000 | 712,000 |
| | Profit improvement (p.a.) | 355,000 |
| *Initial investment* | | |
| Advertising and brochures for new insurance plan | 226,000 | |
| Recruitment and training of 52 clerks | 67,000 | |
| Training agents | 60,000 | |
| Systems design and program development | 250,000 | |
| Offices (furniture, etc.) | 34,000 | |
| | | 637,000 |

INVESTMENT RECOVERY PERIOD

$$\frac{\$637,000}{\$354,000} = 1.8 \text{ years}$$

This is a simple example but it illustrates the essential points, namely:

**(a) Start with the benefit.** This computer system was not introduced to "save money." Management studied their opportunities and realized that they could increase their share of the life insurance market. They identified their main weakness as ineffective selling by their agents.

The corporation decided to introduce a new type of life policy, with certain novel and attractive features for the policyholder. A main feature of this new policy, however, was to be the ease of selling it from the agent's point of view. The corporation found that, if certain calculations and information handling could be done in their offices, the agent's work could be greatly simplified, and also the proposal could be made much more attractive to the customer, regarding both the benefit to be offered and the way in which he paid his premiums. Armed with this new type of insurance and the simplified proposal forms and payments system, the sales director accepted as his personal objective an increase in the level of annual premiums paid such that annual gross profit would increase by $1,068,000.

**(b) Cost of the total plan for achieving the benefit.** The achievement of this new business depended on a new system of accepting proposals, calculating premiums, and accepting payments—which, in turn, necessitated more calculations and processing being done by the office. The corporation felt that they would be unable to recruit enough people to do this work. More important, supervising such a large number of clerks would involve management problems which they did not feel able to handle. Furthermore, space to accommodate a large clerical work force would be very costly, and the accuracy and complexity of the calculations and the speed of processing demanded by the new system were probably beyond what could be expected from any clerical system. This new scheme was a practical proposition only if a computer-based data processing system were to be used.

The cost of this system—including hardware, data preparation, systems design, and programming—was worked out (the fact that they used a computer service bureau is not, of course, relevant to the argument). The discipline of setting a measured improvement on this objective, however, forced management to consider and to cost all the measures they would need to take to achieve this objective. In addition to costing the computer system, which was only a part of the plan, they also costed the training of their agents to sell the new policies, the advertising needed, the design and printing of new brochures, etc.

## Stage 5.  Implement system

In this stage, the systems are designed in detail, and computer programs are written, tested, and put on the machine. These tasks are usually carried out largely by project teams, and we shall deal with this in detail in Part 3, "The Efficient Computer Department."

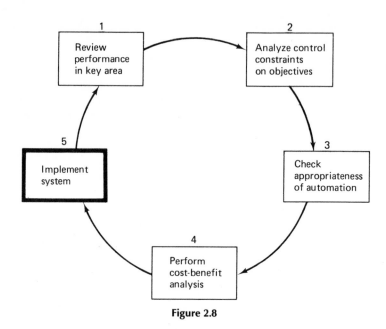

**Figure 2.8**

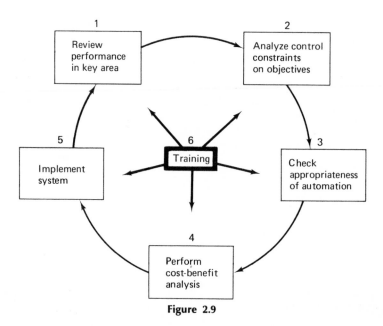

**Figure 2.9**

## Stage 6. Training

This stage concerns the training of computer staff, the computer users, and management in the company. It is of paramount importance, and is also dealt with in Part 3. We stress at this point that training is not a separate stage in this approach. It is shown in the center of Figure 2.9 to illustrate the point that it takes place continually, and mainly on the job, as part of the participation and special involvement of the computer staff and users in the effective use of computers fostered by this approach.

# Review

Review of the performance of the computer department itself, and review of the progress of implementation by the project team in stage 5, are both dealt with in Part 3. There are two other vital aspects of review, however, which we deal with now.

The cycle of stages in the effective computer approach are drawn in a circle to show that they are repeated at regular intervals. Repetition of stage 1 achieves a regular appraisal of how far the company has gone toward achieving its objectives. Remember that these were set as measured targets at the outset ("to reduce work in progress by $33,600," "to reduce distribution costs by $528,000," "to increase profits by $204,000"). Each time we review performance in the key areas, we measure to what degree these objectives have been achieved. The discipline of measuring this progress enables us to discover whether the objective is still feasible, whether the users' plans should be altered, and whether the computer system should be altered.

▶ A carpet manufacturer had the objective of increasing profitability. The plan for achieving this included direct sale to the customer, inventory reduction, waste reduction on cutting, and improved debt collection. A new computer system for accounting, inventory, and production control was also planned. In this case:

Inventory reductions proved impossible, since they conflicted with the manufacturer's "direct sale" policy. which involved keeping the stocks previously held by the wholesalers.

No mathematical solution was found that would improve the cutting strategy.

Debt collection did not improve, since the system was in conflict with the policy of allowing credit to boost the "direct sale" strategy, and was not, therefore, enforced.

The computer system employed open-item accounting and, even during three shifts, it could not be processed on the equipment ordered, and further capacity had to be bought from a service bureau.

These four failures could have been predicted early on and fresh plans made. No measured objectives were set, however, either for profit improvement or for the detailed contributory plans and systems. Progress reviews consisted of uncoordinated opinions of how things were going. There were no yardsticks against which to judge performance, and the computer project, which lasted three years, was allowed to continue unaltered.

Secondly, the repetition of stage 1 ensures that the review of the company's overall control system takes place continually. This is necessary because new key areas emerge as the organization evolves. Furthermore, within the old key areas, new problems arise, constraints disappear, further possibilities for using the computer emerge, and the progress made by automation itself creates new ideas. These factors cause us to consider fresh possibilities for automation each time we go round the cycle—and also to consider removing certain procedures from the computer from time to time.

▶ A corporation manufacturing chemicals and gases identified a key area as liquidity. It set an objective of reducing its average age of accounts receivable from 4.2 months' sales to 3.3 months'. It recognized that its clerks were overburdened with keeping the accounts accurately (a routine task unsuitable for human beings) and could not give time to dealing with customer queries (a judgment task for which humans are specially suited). As part of its plan for the reduction of accounts receivable (which included a reorganization of sales divisions into regions), a computer-based accounting system was implemented. Two years later, management reexamined the key area of liquidity. The average age of accounts receivable had now fallen to 3.6 months. It was seen that most customer queries related to chargeable gas cylinders. It was decided that separate invoices should be sent out for these items, thus avoiding the delaying of the whole invoice. This was a high-volume repetitive job, again unsuitable for a human control system but perfectly practicable for an automated system. This new system was then implemented, and the accounts receivable fell to 2.9 months.

The third time round the cycle, the company recognized a new key area, "cylinder control." The investment tied up in gas cylinders had increased by over $1.2 million in the last two years. Although theoretically they were chargeable, customers disputed that they had still got these cylinders, and the automated control system—which followed the practice of the clerical system it replaced—did not identify the location of cylinders, and therefore no claim could be pressed. The objective set was to reduce this investment by $720,000 within four years. A cylinder identification and control system, too bulky and complex to handle by humans, was designed and implemented. The system enabled the company substantially to achieve its objective within the first three years of operation.

# Implementing the approach

The essence of this approach, and at the same time its main difficulty, is to involve the user of the computer system in a constructive analysis of how the computer can help him to achieve improvements; also, to commit the user to cooperate in an overall plan (of which the new computer system is only a part) to achieve this benefit. This difficulty is widely understood in firms using computers—witness the frequent strategy referred to earlier of "charging the user," and also, the fact that the most commonly attributed cause of disappointment is "lack of management participation."

There are many different ways of trying to overcome this problem. Two of them, described in the remainder of Part 2, have been found most successful in practice.

### 1. The systems adviser

Those familiar with the "MBO adviser" concept will immediately recognize the basis of this idea. A man, trained in the effective computer approach, sits down with each of the senior managers in the company, individually or in groups. The adviser is invariably an experienced computer systems analyst. He will discuss the key areas of the company with each manager, and identify the objectives the manager has in each of them. They analyze together how the present control system constrains the manager in achieving these objectives, and how the possibilities offered by automation might overcome the constraints and enable him to set higher objectives.

> ▶ A corporation manufacturing glass products had had a computer installed for five years. They had not succeeded in achieving significant business benefits from computer data processing. To overcome this disappointment, they were considering installing a computer-based management information system. As a first step, the systems analysts in the corporation asked the managers what information they wanted. They found, with some surprise, that the managers did not know. After consideration, however, they realized that no manager would be able to provide an immediate constructive answer to this question. If he felt a need for information and was a competent manager, he would either have satisfied this need or

| Key area | Key decisions | Scope for improvement | Information needed to obtain improvement | Quantification of benefit, i.e., new objectives possible with this information |
|---|---|---|---|---|
| Negotiation of business | 1. Which market and which customer to go for. | Sales plans based on opportunity at present, i.e., passive marketing. But sales of bottles are tied to sale of the product itself, which is frequently predictable. We can influence our share of these markets and change to an active marketing strategy. | Market trends and product forecasts. Production feasibility and profitability of alternative strategies. | Profit improvement of $360,000–$480,000. |
| | 2. Whether to accept a particular contract (yes/no decisions and choice between alternatives). | Decisions "opportunity based" at present. Could be based on the effect on profitability of accepting one order rather than another (volume is not necessarily the best criterion). Improve job mix by shuffling the order book based on profitability. | Profitability and "contribution" of each product/volume. Effect of accepting contract on overall profit plan. | |
| | 3. What price to charge. | Based on competition and "what market will bear" at present. Could also consider effect on overall profitability of order book. We need to adopt a "discriminatory" pricing policy so that we can use it in bargaining. | Profitability and "contribution" at various prices. Effect of prices on overall sales volume by product. | Profit improvement of $240,000. |

| | | | | |
|---|---|---|---|---|
| Budgeting and planning | 1. Setting objectives for each product by market and major customer. | Identifying scope for profit improvement in each market and product group, testing to make sure plans are feasible, attempting to optimize plans toward the most profitable strategy, and "putting teeth into MBO" by settling on realistic targets with management. Plans at present are based on adjustments to last year's achievement rather than a complete rethink. | Feasibility and profitability of alternative strategies. Answers to "what if" questions concerning marketing and production strategies. | Market share increase from 23 to 28 per cent. Profit improvement $960,000. |
| | 2. Revising objectives in the light of performance. | At present, plans are made once a year and then fixed. We need to monitor the situation and make changes in plans as our needs become clear. | Performance review against each manager's objectives, with prediction of future performance based on how things are going at present. Answer to "what if" questions concerning fresh marketing and production strategies. | |
| Customer contact | When to contact major customers. | Could be based on our stock-holding position for our "proprietary brand" customers and "specially packed goods" customers. Our stocks would be used as a sales tool to get them to "call off" further supplies. We could charge for holding stocks. | For each proprietary brand and specially packed product: i. stocks ii. estimated customer orders iii. what he has actually ordered. | Inventory reduction of $360,000. Sales volume increase of $504,000. |

etc.

Manager: Mr. Floggit, to marketing manager; date: April 14, 1971

**Figure 2.10**

adopted a management style that enabled him to achieve satisfactory results without it. Two systems advisers were appointed, therefore, who carried out the following analysis with each manager.

i.   analyze key areas;
ii.  analyze objectives in each key area;
iii. analyze the information needed to meet these objectives;
iv.  assess benefits to be obtained by providing this information (calculated as the difference between the manager's objectives achievable with and without the improved information).

Management responded positively to this analysis. The key area "budgeting and planning" was identified as one yielding the most significant benefits, and a computer-based business model was constructed to assist the management team in planning and in assessing the effect of their plans on the corporation's budget. An $864,000 improvement in profitability was achieved, largely attributable to improved planning.

Equally important, the constructive cooperation between computer analyst and management led subsequently to the adoption of the objective of reducing distribution costs by $264,000 and a computer-based scheduling and control system was designed and implemented as part of the plan to achieve this objective.

The form shown in Figure 2.10 was used by the systems adviser in this company.

## 2. Computer task force[2]

A task force is a means of bringing together a number of managers to make a concerted determination of the course of action to be taken in a critical area of the corporation's activities. It should not be confused with a committee, which is often used as a means of improving coordination.

Committees are often made up of individuals who are furthering or protecting sectional interests and such a body is largely concerned with the balancing of conflicting objectives. A task force is concerned with the identification and setting of common objectives.

The computer task force is appointed specifically to perform stages 1, 2, 3, and 4 of the effective computer approach. There can be a separate computer task force for each key area if necessary. The task force is a small group—preferably not less than four nor more than six—whose members are chosen because they each have a particular contribution to make to the determination of the course of action and/or its subsequent implementation. Members of the task force should be of three kinds:

(a) Persons with knowledge and experience of the particular activity. The authority of the task force rests on their depth of knowledge of the subject under investigation. The members should be regarded as the corporation's leading authorities on the facets of management involved. In addition, at least one member must provide authority on computing feasibility and implications. He may be the data processing manager, a senior analyst, a senior programmer, or an outsider. The point is that a task force will fail if it reaches decisions without sufficient knowledge of the relevant facts.

(b) Persons who are line managers involved in implementing the decisions. Again, experience shows that the task force will fail if the line managers responsible for securing the improvement in the key area being studied are told of the task force's decision after it has been made, rather than being involved in forming its decisions.

(c) Persons with appropriate skill in analytical and investigatory techniques—for example, methods engineers, systems analysts, etc.

It is important to secure a balance of these aspects of knowledge, involvement, and skill. Status within the organization hierarchy is not a selection criterion, and the team will frequently consist of managers, supervisors, and computer staff drawn from different management levels. They represent what has been termed a diagonal slice of the organization structure, but disparity of rank and status in the team rarely gives rise to complications, so long as each member is seen to have an important contribution to make.

A notable feature of computer task force exercises has been the concept of a "team manager," who has either been a consultant or the corporation's management by objectives adviser. His role is important to the successful introduction of a regular and continuing computer task force.

While not himself participating in the actual investigation, he performs the following functions:

(a) he helps to identify the appropriate areas for investigation and the type of task force operation to use;

(b) he assists in the selection and preliminary training of the team;

(c) he guides the team in the systematic method of analysis to be used;

(d) he advises the team on their form of presentation;

(e) he ensures that the agreed objectives for the computer are incorporated into the user's unit improvement plan.

## CLIMATE REQUIRED

The company should first have identified its key areas. While the computer task force could, at any time, carry out an investigation of any part of the business *without* a framework of key areas and a procedural discipline, the timing and choice of such investigations becomes a matter of chance, usually governed by fire-fighting needs. The identification of the key areas may itself be a task force exercise, however. More important, therefore, are the following three factors:

**1. Management style.** For participation to have any meaning, it must essentially be "participation with the boss," who must be prepared to share his thinking and decision making with his subordinates and to make frequent contact with them. The change in behavior must, therefore, start with the head of the unit, and where this is unlikely to be achieved (e.g., some executives have personalities which preclude such a permissive style of leadership), true participation at lower levels within the unit will not be successful.

Experience also suggests that high degrees of order, harmony, and discipline within the enterprise are preconditional requirements rather than postconditional effects of a participative system of management. The sudden involvement of people who have previously and habitually performed a dependent role is unlikely to bring order out of chaos, harmony out of discord. Note that "the boss" means the chief executive—and also the boss of any subunit within the company where a computer-assisted improvement is being sought.

**2. Atmosphere of confidence.** The current level of self-esteem of the management team, born of the success of the enterprise, is also a factor determining the extent to which participation is appropriate. A corporation which has an air of confidence arising from a growing demand for its products or services, and which feels it is going places, is more likely to provide the right environment than one which has an air of despair arising from an outdated range of products, and which clings to the fact that it has been places as the dubious basis of its self-respect. We have said that, for computers to fulfill their strategic role, they must help the corporation to achieve new objectives. In the absence of a confident atmosphere, they are more likely to be used for the doubtful objective of reducing the costs of existing systems.

Even more important perhaps, in this connection, is the level of self-esteem of the computer staff, and the confidence which the corporation has in its computer department. Does the computer department feel it is going places? Do users initiate a high level of demand for its services? Or is the machine discredited, and further applications resisted by users?

Are the computer staff considered "separate" from the rest of the organization? If the latter attitude continues after the computer has been installed for more than a year or two, then experience shows that the computer department itself needs improvement. Targets are probably not being met, wanted changes in the system are not being made, computer outputs are unsatisfactory, costs are not under control, etc. No computer task force can hope to succeed in this atmosphere. The user's participation should not be invited until the computer house itself is put in order. (This is dealt with in detail in Part 3.)

**3. Perception of the computer.** If the men who matter in the corporation believe that the computer's role is to reduce administrative costs, the climate will work against the creative analysis and thinking needed to identify business improvements that will be made possible if control constraints are altered. Furthermore, it is unlikely that the right men will be assigned to the computer task force, or that its decisions will be backed.

The function of the computer task force is to add to or modify the computer's objectives. (Remember that the task force's findings are only arrived at through a process of discussion and challenge, leading to agreement with their ideas by others involved.)

A computer task force study may involve a substantial investment in manager-hours—and there may need to be several studies undertaken within one unit. This is a large amount of valuable management time. It is important, therefore, that the task force should never be allowed to prolong a particular study and turn itself into a committee. Their function is complete when they have derived some objectives and formulated a plan of action. They should not, *as a team*, be concerned with implementation.

There is no one best way of structuring a computer task force operation. The danger of using a ready-made, problem-solving technique is that it may not meet the particular requirements of the situation, or suit the particular style of management within the unit. It is inadvisable to put creative thinking into too formal a straitjacket. Nevertheless, the following basic steps have to be taken:

> *Step 1.* Establish which aspects of the firm's operations might be improved by the removal or alleviation of present control constraints—i.e., identify the key areas to be studied.
> *Step 2.* Set up a series of difficult but desirable goals for improving results in the key areas identified.

| Key result area | What we want to achieve | What control constraints prevent us from obtaining it? | Check other contraints. Can these be removed? | What prevents us from using human beings satisfactorily to overcome the control constraints? | How can computer control overcome the constraint—or help humans to overcome it? |
|---|---|---|---|---|---|
| Market share | Compensate for decline in the wholesale market by providing a service to tradesmen and do-it-yourself market. | i. Volume increase in order processing (more orders of lower volume). | | i. Present staff shortage. Could not increase numbers to cope with higher volumes. No increase in turnover to pay for more staff; no space to accommodate them. | i. Volume increase has less effect on cost and space. |
| | | ii. Complex discounting, pricing, and inducement schemes required. | | ii. Complexity of the system would require an unacceptable amount of training—and slow up work. | ii. Once rules are programmed, training problems are removed. Complex rules will not affect speed of processing. |
| | | iii. Speed of order processing. | Fast delivery service of small orders (24 hours). | iii. Communication between order-taking and order-processing and stock-control clerks could not be accomplished in time. | iii. These three processes will be integrated within the one machine. |
| | | iv. Accurate forecasting of orders. | High stock levels (wholesalers carry our stocks for us at present). | iv. Sufficient accuracy on a large volume of data on a continuing routine basis is beyond the capacity of human beings. | iv. Machine's powers of logical manipulation can provide human beings with statistically accurate forecasts. |

**Figure 2.11**

Step 3. Identify the control constraints which prevent or hamper the achievement of these improvements.

Step 4. Check whether other obstacles exist which prevent or hamper their achievement, and whether these can be overcome.

Step 5. Analyze why human control systems have not already overcome these control obstacles (identified in step 3).

Step 6. Analyze why computer control would overcome or help to overcome them.

The analysis sheet of Figure 2.11 illustrates this approach. It is taken from a computer task force working in a wallpaper manufacturing company, facing a decline in wholesale business. Note that column 3 describes a goal which has not yet been formulated into an "objective" in the MBO sense—i.e., it is not yet expressed as a *measured* improvement (viz., increase DIY orders to $3.6 million in the next 18 months). Note also that there will normally be other constraints, in addition to control, which will have to be overcome (column 5). The solution of these constraints sometimes gives rise to further control constraints, as in this case.

## Company organization structure and the computer

The effectiveness of the computer is certainly influenced by its correct location in the firm's organization structure. In making this decision, there is an important underlying point of principle for the corporation to settle. The computer department can be regarded as a source of neutral, professional advice to which line management may refer problems, invite comments, etc. This is a passive but influential role in which the computer department's power comes from technical knowledge and lack of bias or "political" commitment. Alternatively, the department can be expected to take a positive initiative in securing innovations of business importance. This is an active role, implying the use of special knowledge to "sell" concepts and methods felt to be worthwhile by computer people. It can arouse antagonism as well as enthusiasm . . . but at least it creates some vitality and argument.

Incidentally, if the *first* viewpoint is accepted, it is unreasonable to accuse the computer department of not being profit oriented. We favor the active role.

Whatever specific choice is made, it is essential to have a careful clarification of objectives for the computer unit, and particularly to clarify its relationships with user departments. Perhaps more than any other department, the computer group cannot survive, let alone flourish, in a vacuum. The success of the new group will depend a good deal on the organizational "culture" and "style" of the rest of the business. Rigidity, bureaucracy, subunits that are defensive about their role and authority— these are all likely to make a new computer department's task difficult, since by definition it is innovative, cuts across traditional departmental boundaries with information flows, and demands participation and team- work as a style.

A great deal has been said about the influence of the computer on the existing organization, and the idea that middle management jobs would in many cases disappear, and a high degree of centralization of power follow, has been widely discussed. So far, in practice, we observe very little effect by the computer on management manning levels—maybe because it has not yet been fully utilized on management problems! The most comprehensive recent study,[3] by Rosemary Stewart, points out that most of the effects on management, with the exception of those on a few junior management jobs, are classifiable as minimal or marginal ones. Certainly, our experience confirms the danger of generalization. For example, for every case in which the potential for centralized power has been demonstrated, there is another in which the computer has for the first time given middle and junior management good information, so that true accountability can be passed to them.

One effect of computer data processing has been to highlight the difference between two forms of control: human control and mechanized control. We may expect the computer to influence future organization structure so that it reflects this distinction. For example, in each function there may be one manager concerned with discretionary control and another responsible for its formal or reflex control systems.

The alternative to this is to give the responsibility for the reflex control area within each function to the computer department. Many companies adopt an uneasy compromise in this respect:

> ► A bank, having computerized its accounts, nominally left all the responsi-
> bility for their maintenance with the branch managers. The branch managers
> were not, in fact, responsible for account accuracy, for making regular
> payments as instructed by customers, or for the provision of statements.
> While they became much more effective regarding the discretionary aspect
> of their work (selling the bank's services, etc.), they lost much of their
> authority concerning routine control to the computer center manager.

Occasionally, however, we find organization structures which recognize the two separate forms of control but retain responsibility for both within the line function concerned.

> ► A chain of retail stores automated part of its buying procedures. This mechanization of routine buying allowed buyers to concentrate on getting the best prices, i.e., on discretionary control. However, the purchasing manager appointed two managers under him, a chief buyer responsible for negotiating contracts and a buying systems manager responsible for developing the rules covering routine work.

Perhaps the most important question for the large concern is whether to include the computer as part of a corporate information department. Since it is natural to assign the computer initially to the manager who makes the most use of it, it is not surprising that most computer installations lie initially in either the accounting or financial controller's departments. As the computer's contribution grows, it is argued that a separate information department should be responsible for identifying the information needs for all levels of management for both planning and control purposes. Moreover, it would develop the necessary systems (which would invariably include computer systems, but not these alone) to fulfill these needs. Although there would be an overlap with, say, accounting and other functions, that would not prevent the information department from making an important contribution.

Professor J. Dearden, however, takes a different view,[4] and states that in actual business situations, systems responsibility has been less successful when centralized. Many systems are already well established, working satisfactorily, and require no "design." Moreover, some important systems have virtually no overlap; each requires different types of knowledge skills, and experience.

It is easier, say, to give a budget man enough knowledge of the computer to work with it, than to teach a computer man enough to design a budgetary control system. His conclusion is that systems specifications should be decentralized. In contrast, however, Dearden strongly recommends that the data processing activity should, and can, be centralized.

> ► Massey-Ferguson Ltd, a major multinational business, is a case[5] in which a separate MIS function has been established, reporting at corporate level to the president. Without this, it is claimed, a truly impartial service to other functions cannot be provided. Equally important is the fact that top management accepts responsibility for goal setting and direction of management information, ensures the direct participation of senior user management in the definition of systems, and makes a clear statement of the user management's accountability for the results of the systems. In Massey-Ferguson, the MIS function is accountable for:
>
> 1. Systems and procedures.
> 2. Operations research.

3. All aspects of data processing and data communication.
4. Those aspects of engineering and manufacturing automation involving the direct application of computers.

Underlying the detailed methods are three basic philosophies entirely compatible with our approach to the effective computer:

The user is accountable to top management for results.

The MIS function is accountable to the *user* management for systems design and technical feasibility.

No proposal is to be approved unless countersigned by both user and MIS management.

## Conclusion

A business which aims to make its computer effective must really understand what the computer can and cannot do well in management terms. This has nothing to do with the complex technical jargon and specifications used by the specialist electronic engineers. Once this understanding is adequate, the really strategic uses of the computer can be analyzed. As we wrote in the Preface, there are three vital principles:

Technical objectives *per se* are not worth pursuing, e.g., updating stock records on a computer, the creation of a data bank, the installation of a real-time customer inquiry system.

The only valid objective for computers is to assist in achieving defined business improvements which would be impossible or uneconomic without the computer.

Computer users must be committed to the defined improvements and are ultimately responsible for carrying out the plan to achieve them. The computer department alone can only produce computer systems, not business improvements.

### References

1. For a fuller list of searching questions, see John Humble, *Improving Business Results,* McGraw-Hill, 1965.
2. For a full description of the task force concept, see the chapter on "Task Force and Management by Objectives," by P. A. Hives in *Management by Objectives in Action,* edited by J. W. Humble, McGraw-Hill, 1970.
3. Rosemary Stewart, *How Computers Affect Management,* Macmillan, 1971.
4. J. Dearden, How to Organize Information Systems, *Harvard Business Review,* vol. 43, 1965, pp. 65–73.
5. See "Management of Information Systems in a Global Corporation," *Business Quarterly,* Autumn 1971.

# Part 3
# The efficient computer department

## Introduction

In Part 2, we considered the role of computers in organizations. We put forward the view that many installations had concentrated on solving the technical problems involved in getting the machine to do a particular job, rather than on identifying the right job for the machine to do. We said that, while the solution of these technical problems represented a truly remarkable achievement in many cases, most computers were a source of some disappointment to general management, who were looking for business improvements. We then considered methods for making computers contribute to business results; in short, Part 2 concentrated on making computers more *effective*. In Part 3 we are going to deal with making computer departments *efficient*. Let us first draw the distinction between effectiveness and efficiency.

In this context, by "effective" we mean usefully contributing to the results of the business or organization. By "efficient" we mean managing the computer department well.

Clearly, the internal management of the department can be considered separately from the overall role the computer plays in the business. It is possible, for example, to find an extremely well-managed and efficient computer department which is, in fact, losing money for the corporation. (The group of companies mentioned in Part 2, whose computer system caused the accounts receivable to rise to the point where the group was in financial difficulty, possessed an extremely well-run installation.) More important, however, it is of little use trying to raise the status of the computer department to the strategic level of assisting in corporate profit improvement plans if the department is not yet running efficiently; if projects are not completed on time, and within cost budgets; if forecasted running costs cannot be achieved; if users are dissatisfied with the service provided.

While this book is primarily concerned with making computers effective, we must also ensure that the computer department runs efficiently. The president, or managing director, who takes a cold and critical look at the department itself is likely to find such things as:

> No clearly defined and up to date objectives for the department. A recent study of 36 US companies showed that 14 had no overall plan for computer applications, and the economic and operational feasibility of individual projects was seldom fully explored. Twenty-four of the 36 companies had not established adequate short-term objectives against which to measure the progress of individual computer projects.

> An inadequate interface between the computer's work and that of the departments it serves.

> A computer that was placed in the total organization structure by historic accident—e.g., reporting to the accountant because payroll was the first application—rather than by carefully considered design.

> Confusion within the department between the *activities* people carry out and the *results* they should achieve.

> Poor internal review and control methods.

> Overconcern with technology and underconcern with profits.

Of course, the best computer installations have a radically different appearance, and only the worst would plead guilty to all six charges! Yet our consulting experience points to the uncomfortable truth that these sins beset most computer installations to a worrying extent.

One explanation may be that the computer is thought about as a new and formidably complex "thing" which it would be unreasonable to subject prematurely to normal critical business analysis.

> We're still living through the teething problems of installation.

> You have to be patient and see the computer as a major "act of faith" type of investment in the early years. The benefits will come later.

> According to the computer manufacturer our performance, managerially and technically, is up to the standard of other similar installations.

> It's so difficult to get high-quality specialists for the computer department that one has to be particularly careful not to upset them.

These are the sort of persuasive comments which lull everyone into a comfortably complacent frame of mind. A special danger of this complacency is that when company profits fall the computer department may be the first to be cut back—a backlash unjustified by its *true* potential but understandable in the light of its past practical achievements.

Another explanation frequently offered for the low efficiency of computer departments is that technical excellence rather than management ability is rewarded by promotion. Certainly, one can find installations where the best specialists hold the senior management positions. It is only by luck if such people also happen to have management skill, with the result that much of the department is badly managed. Also valuable specialist skills are lost, since the more-able systems analysts and programmers have been promoted to allegedly "higher things"!

## An MBO approach to improving efficiency

In seeking to improve the efficiency of computer departments, we shall describe a management by objectives approach. We have found this approach to be particularly suitable for computer staff. As we have seen, MBO employs a style of management in which, to a large extent, people control themselves. As is to be expected, intelligent and responsible "knowledge people" respond well to this approach. By way of introduction, and before we get down to the details of how we introduce MBO into a computer department, let us define the most important terms and concepts which MBO employs.

PURPOSE. Purpose, in the MBO sense, means answering the question "What customer needs are we trying to satisfy?" Contrast this with another use of the word which answers the question "What do *we* want to achieve?" and which is *not* the MBO concept at all.

POLICY. A policy is a self-imposed constraint on the business—something which we have said we will or will not do, and which we abide by in deciding our detailed strategies and tactics.

KEY AREAS. These are the few areas which are really vital in meeting our purpose. Of all the areas of activity which go on in a corporation, the key areas are those few in which good or bad performance significantly affects our results.

OBJECTIVES. An objective is a statement of an intended and measured improvement.

PERFORMANCE STANDARDS. Like an objective, a performance standard is a statement of an intended and measured level of performance, but it does not represent an improvement in the sense that special action must be taken to achieve it—it is rather a level of performance we are seeking to maintain.

KEY TASKS. Of all the things that an individual does, his key tasks are those few which, done well or badly, will determine whether he achieves his objectives or performance standards. Distinguish key tasks from key areas. Key areas are relevant at corporate or departmental level and are the areas in which key tasks are performed.

RESULTS GUIDES. A results guide is a document prepared together by a man and his boss describing, among other things, the man's objectives and performance standards for the next review period.

REVIEW. Review is the process of examining measured performance against objectives and performance standards, considering action to take in the light of performance, and setting fresh objectives and performance standards. The process of review, which may also involve identifying new key areas and key tasks, thus makes MBO a dynamic process. The whole continuing process is illustrated in the diagram in the Preface.

We have divided our description of the application of MBO to computer departments into four stages as follows:

    Initial study
    Preparation of results guides
    Task forces
    Review

## Initial study

Before introducing MBO into the computer department, it is necessary to undertake an initial study. This study should seek to accomplish five things.

### 1. Appointing advisers

The role of the adviser, when introducing MBO, has been found to be of great importance. The adviser, in fact, "manages" the exercise during its first year. By the end of the year, the new approach to management should have taken root and his services can frequently be dispensed with. His chief functions are:

> To carry out the preliminary study, advising on preliminary work, purpose, and key areas.
>
> To prepare plans for the introduction of MBO including discussion schedules and the times for the preparation of results guides.
>
> To be present at boss/subordinate meetings and task force meetings, acting both as an adviser on the concepts and practice of MBO and as an outside catalyst giving a third party's view, challenging some of the "standard objections" to improvements, and generally facilitating open and free discussion (which the established hierarchy and organizational framework can sometimes inhibit). At these meetings, he will assist in formulating objectives and action plans, and undertake some of the clerical work.

The adviser is often appointed from inside the organization, but preferably from outside the computer department. It is essential that he has experience with MBO, since he will be explaining its principles and practice to staff who are invariably not familiar with it. For this reason, a consultant who is an experienced practitioner is often employed to start off the exercise, and the internal adviser is trained to take over after several months. To give an idea of the number of advisers and time scales required, the following two cases may be found helpful.

▶ A large computer department employing 860 staff (including systems and procedures and methods, engineering staff, systems analysts, programmers, computer operators, and data preparation staff) appointed three internal advisers and retained an MBO consultant. In one year these four men completed the initial study, the preparation of results guides for all senior staff, six task force exercises, and a first review. (The consultant was employed part time for the last four months.)

▶ A computer department employing

One senior manager
Three systems analysts
Seven programmers
Six data control staff
Eight operating staff
Thirteen data preparation staff

retained a consultant for four months to perform the initial study, draw up results guides for eight senior people, and train one of their staff as an internal adviser. At the end of four months, the internal adviser took over and worked for one day a week for the rest of the year on two task forces, and on performance and key task review.

## 2. Preliminary work

It is sometimes necessary to do some preliminary work to "clear the decks" before the department can devote the time and attention to MBO that its introduction requires. This work usually consists of finishing some project or putting right some problem which is demanding all the department's attention at the time.

▶ A year after installing a computer, a publishing house decided to introduce MBO throughout the organization, including the computer department. This department was already two months behind with its second major project in the periodicals accounts. The computer was underutilized and waiting for this extra work; the accounts department was under great pressure, having transferred its accounts onto computer files, and having to maintain both the computer records and the manual records by hand. Although a success in the rest of the firm, MBO failed in the computer department since all the staff had the urgent priority of getting "periodicals" going as quickly as possible, and only went through the motions as far as analyzing their departmental work and setting objectives for improvement were concerned.

▶ A county council decided to use MBO in its computer department. During the preliminary study, carried out by the MBO adviser and the data processing manager, the utilization of the computer was analyzed. This machine was of recent design and employed a novel random access device and a certain amount of untested software. It was found that the access time per record was nearly three times greater than had been estimated, and that further work due for transfer onto the computer in six weeks' time would seriously overload the equipment. It was decided to carry out certain preliminary work, therefore, before embarking on the MBO exercise proper. Two programs were rewritten to allow file amendment to take place at the same time as file updating, thus avoiding one complete pass through the taxpayers' file. Also, arrangements were made to work a third shift for the first two weeks of each month. This preliminary work solved a problem that, had it been allowed to continue, would have diverted the attention of the important computer staff when MBO was being introduced.

## 3. Defining purposes

Having appointed the MBO adviser and satisfied ourselves that there is no crisis which will prevent the department from devoting sufficient time to the MBO exercise, the first thing to do is establish the purpose of the department. We have already defined purpose as "our customers' needs." Careful thought about our customers' needs will ensure that objectives are based securely on satisfying these needs, rather than on the insecure basis of satisfying only what we want to do. It should provide us with some insight into what business we are really in.

▶ An ocean liner corporation facing competition from airlines defined its purpose as "to provide business and vacation passengers with pleasurable travel facilities." The thinking behind the word "pleasurable" gained them the insight that they were really in the entertainment as well as travel business, which had a profound effect on their future plans and objectives.

If we do not first establish their purpose, the key areas we subsequently identify will just be a list of areas which seem to be important because a lot of activity goes on there. We are after those areas which really contribute to our success.

There are two purposes for a computer installation: *ultimate purpose* and *proximate purpose*. See Figure 3.1.

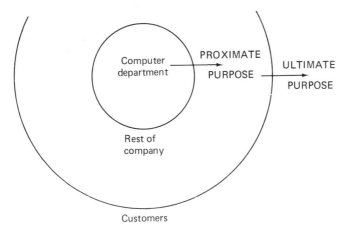

**Figure 3.1**

The computer department's ultimate purpose is the same as the corporation's overall purpose, and is concerned with the needs of the corporation's customers.

We have italicized those words in the examples in Figure 3.2 which lead the firm concerned to change its activities as a result of thinking about its purpose.

The key areas we identify, with the firm's ultimate purpose in mind, will enable us to set objectives for the company which concentrate on getting it to contribute to improving the company's performance—to make the computer more *effective*. We described this approach in Part 2.

We can also identify a proximate purpose for the computer, however.

| Company | Examples of ultimate purpose | Resultant new activities |
|---|---|---|
| Airline | To provide a fast and *complete* international transport service for people and goods | Transporting to and from airports |
| Paint and decorating materials manufacturer | To provide materials and *methods* for tradesmen and the *public* to decorate the inside and outside of buildings | Making easy-to-use products for the do-it-yourself market |
| Brewery | To meet the *leisure* time needs of the UK market | Improving public houses as social centers |

**Figure 3.2**

This describes the needs of the computer's immediate customers, i.e., the user departments in the rest of the firm. The key areas we identify with this purpose in mind will cause us to concentrate on providing a more *efficient* computer service—which is our goal in Part 3.

Again, in Figure 3.3, the words we have italicized provided some insight for the firms concerned. Note that a statement of purpose, in addition to defining customers' needs, should also state who those customers are.

| Company | Examples of computer department's proximate purpose | Resultant new activities |
|---|---|---|
| Bank | To *assist line management* in <br> 1. Clarifying the scope and objectives for the design and review of systems and associated job structure. <br> 2. Designing, purchasing, implementing, and operating systems to meet those objectives. <br> 3. Reviewing the organization of work and job structure to manage and operate those systems. <br> 4. Training staff in respect to the above to achieve optimum benefits. | Involving users in initial studies and arranging for the benefits of computer systems to be incorporated into users' objectives. |
| Oil corporation | To provide a *formal* system for issuing instructions and information to members of the company and outsiders. | Setting up an in-house training course on the significance of, and the distinction between, formal (or reflex) control and discretionary control. |

**Figure 3.3**

The most succinct description of purpose we have come across for a computer department is:

> To enable users to obtain business benefits.

## 4. Defining policies

Next, we examine the policies for the computer department. There are three main reasons for examining policy at this stage. Firstly, a clear understanding of policy now will prevent us from later setting objectives and plans for improvement which are unacceptable to the corporation. Secondly, since policies are self-imposed, careful examination of the reason for their existence may cause us to reconsider whether they are right. Thirdly, we may discover significant omissions which in turn cause the department to refer too many decisions upward and delay progress.

▶ A well-known software house adopted the policy of employing women only. This policy greatly benefited the company by giving it excellent publicity. The women subsequently agreed to have their remuneration deferred until payment was received from their clients which effectively financed the growth of the company.

▶ A paper manufacturer, having pioneered both second- and third-generation hardware and much of the associated software, discovered that, far from being ahead technically, the work involved in getting new equipment to function properly had put them two years behind in EDP achievement and (they estimated) had doubled their costs. They decided, as a policy, that no further hardware should be purchased which had not been successfully operated by a user in the UK for at least nine months.

It is usual to find that policy is vague and rarely formally stated in computer departments. During the preliminary study, the corporation should seek to clarify its existing policies, for example regarding:

Staff recruitment
Promotion
Salaries
Equipment
Justification
Automation, etc.

The ground is thus prepared for any policy alterations and additions where the need shows up during the MBO exercise proper.

## 5. SWOT analysis

The initials SWOT stand for strengths, weaknesses, opportunities, and threats. An analysis of these four factors with regard to the computer department has frequently been found very helpful, in order subsequently to identify the key areas for improvement.

> ► A large engineering company had used computers for nine years. As part of their preliminary study for MBO in the computer department, they identified the strengths and weaknesses in the department (shown in Figure 3.4) and also the opportunities and threats which faced them from outside the department.

| Strengths | Weaknesses | Opportunities | Threats |
|---|---|---|---|
| 120 systems analysts and programmers | Responsibility for achieving user benefits ill defined | Users now have computer experience | Maintenance will dominate future work and may affect morale among experts |
| Nine years' experience of designing and implementing commercial computer systems | Boundaries of projects ill defined, especially the end | MBO is installed in user departments | Effect of computer and systems failure on business results |
| All systems recently transferred onto the latest equipment | Progress review systems do not reappraise project terms of reference | | User fear of possible takeover of routine administration by management services |
| Over 20 per cent spare capacity on computer processing equipment | Authority of project controller regarding resources is often unclear | | View growing in company, and internationally, that computers do not save money |

**Figure 3.4**   SWOT analysis form. Note that the strengths and weaknesses constitute an *internal* analysis—"what are we, in the computer department, good at and bad at?" Opportunities and threats, on the other hand, form an *external* analysis of the present and potential computer users. Following this analysis, action plans can be formulated to overcome weaknesses and threats by exploiting our strengths and opportunities.

## 6. Identifying key areas

Having defined our purpose and policies, and analyzed our strengths, weaknesses, opportunities, and threats, we are in a position to identify the key areas for the computer department. We want to concentrate our attention on the few areas (usually five or six) in which improvements will have the greatest effect on our present and future efficiency.

▶ During a SWOT analysis, a large financial institution identified a major weakness as lack of user confidence, stemming from failure to produce clearly defined benefits; recent increases in charges to users for computer services; and failure to meet target dates. They also believed that they were threatened by worsening morale among their own technical staff. They identified the following key areas:

   i.   Achievement of benefits from the use of computer department services.
   ii.   Technical innovation.
   iii.   Utilization of resources.
   iv.   Project planning and control.
   v.   Recruitment and training of staff.
   vi.   Staff performance and attitudes.
   vii.   Industrial relations.

▶ Another computer department belonging to a wallpaper manufacturer sought to capitalize on the opportunities they were presented with, following the introduction of MBO in the rest of the company—and the five years' computer experience of the user departments. They believed that the information needed by management could now be identified and a much more beneficial computer system introduced. They also believed that users could participate more in systems analysis. They established the following key areas:

   i.   Data collection and storage.
   ii.   Technical innovations.
   iii.   Programming and operating costs.
   iv.   Technical feasibility.
   v.   Economic justification.

It is important to consider the selection of key areas carefully, since their choice governs much of what we do next. It is not an easy thing to

| General key areas at corporate level | General key areas for computer departments |
|---|---|
| Profitability | Benefits from present operations |
| Innovation | Justification of new applications |
| Productivity | { Operating<br>{ Project development |
| Physical and financial resources | Selection of equipment, software, and services |
| Worker performance and development ⎫<br>Manager performance and development ⎭ | Staff development |
| Market position | Extent of electronic data processing in company |

**Figure 3.5**

do, however. Peter Drucker has stated in general terms the seven key areas for any organization; we list them in Figure 3.5, together with suggested equivalents for computer departments. These may be helpful when starting to think about a particular computer installation.

We emphasize that these are in general terms, however; the description of what is a key area for one computer department is not likely to be true for another. For example, Figure 3.6 shows a selection of key areas we have identified from our work in various computer departments.

| General heading | Examples of key areas |
|---|---|
| Benefit from present operations | Examination of alternatives<br>Examination of use made of outputs<br>Achievement of targets<br>Return on investment<br>Target planning<br>Meeting changed requirements |
| Justification of new applications | Benefit analysis<br>Evaluation of alternatives<br>Defining choice criteria<br>Estimation of computer requirements (time/resources)<br>Feasibility<br>Estimation of development requirements (time/resources)<br>Investigation of side effects<br>Assessment of future scope<br>Exploitation of technical developments<br>Competitive comparisons<br>Analysis of trends affecting automation (cost/sociological) |
| Operating | Work scheduling<br>User service (deadline/errors)<br>Machine utilization<br>Supplies provisioning<br>Operating costs<br>Machine maintenance planning<br>Program efficiency<br>Program breakdown<br>Charging for services<br>Equipment extension, replacement, and rationalization<br>Operating performance standards (machines)<br>Operating methods standards<br>Manpower allocation<br>Utilization of space<br>Insurance of equipment and services<br>Program maintenance methods<br>Standby services<br>Program maintenance performance standards<br>File storage and control<br>Security of files<br>Morale<br>Incentive schemes |

**Figure 3.6**

| General heading | Examples of key areas |
|---|---|
| Operating | Operator/supervisor performance standards<br>Operation control |
| Project development | Activity scheduling<br>Project control<br>Performance standards<br>Methods standards<br>User involvement<br>Liaison with manufacturers<br>Control of subcontractors<br>Manpower allocation<br>User training<br>Justification review<br>Project testing<br>Project development costs<br>Resource allocation<br>User guarantees<br>Cost recovery<br>Morale |
| Selection of equipment, software, and services | Specification of requirements<br>Identifying suppliers<br>Assessing proposals<br>Choice of equipment and software<br>Installation of equipment<br>Financing of equipment<br>Development of alternative suppliers<br>External services |
| Staff development | Assessment of staff requirement<br>Recruitment<br>Performance review<br>Identifying training needs<br>Training<br>Salary structure<br>Succession and career planning<br>Welfare facilities<br>Compliance with statutory regulations<br>Management/employee relations<br>Conditions of employment<br>Organization structure<br>Effective communication<br>Contribution to technical development and education |
| Extent of EDP | Perception of computer's role<br>Long-term planning<br>Selling EDP services<br>Overall procedures review<br>Pricing policy<br>Amount of EDP<br>Distribution of EDP<br>Contribution to business needs<br>Pilot scheme demonstration<br>User relations (PR) |

**Figure 3.6** (contd)

## Preparation of results guides

Having completed the initial study, we can now get down to the next stage of work—the preparation of a results guide for each senior member of the staff in the computer department. This work falls into two stages. One is the preparation of the results guide with the individual concerned. These guides contain objectives and action plans, and, so that the resulting efforts of each person will form a coordinated part of an overall plan to improve the efficiency of the department as a whole, it is essential to perform certain work first. This first stage is concerned with setting objectives for the department as a whole in each key area, and then developing a hierarchy of subobjectives for each individual which represents his contribution to the departmental objective. The plan for preparing results guides, therefore, usually takes the following form:

> *Stage 1.* Set departmental objectives in each key area. Identify key tasks contributing to departmental objectives.
>
> *Stage 2.* Analyze key tasks with the individuals concerned. Set objectives and prepare action plans. Set performance standards. Set up review information systems.

The work involved under each of the headings in Figure 3.6 is described below:

### 1. Set departmental objectives in each key area

While there is no set form for an objective, it should ideally contain the four parts illustrated in Figure 3.7.

| Action | Result | Date | Cost |
|---|---|---|---|
| "to . . ." (a verb) | A measured improvement | The time when the result is to be assessed | The budget for performing the action |
| e.g., *to* reduce the production of a parts explosion | To 95 minutes | By April 1 | Within $3,360 reprogramming costs. (The cost of achieving the objective can often be omitted where the job holder is already working to an agreed budget.) |

**Figure 3.7**

The discipline of defining what we are trying to do with this sort of precision is one that is often resisted at first, but it has been found to be a discipline that leads to *realistic* and *thorough* planning and to a *constructive* review of progress.

The objectives can be summarized in a *computer department action plan*. There is no standard layout for this plan, of course.

▶ One computer department, serving a group of companies in the engineering field, analyzed its objectives for each key area, using the following form:

| Key area | Problems we have to solve | Objectives for 1973 (quantity, quality, time and cost standards) |
| --- | --- | --- |

**Figure 3.8**

They prepared a checklist of headings to help them identify "problems we have to solve" under the three headings of Planning, Project development, and Operating, as in Figure 3.9.

| Planning | Project development | Operating |
| --- | --- | --- |
| Facilities requirements | Initiating ideas for automation | Input control |
| Hardware projection | | Data preparation |
| Survey of new hardware | Preliminary assessment | Scheduling equipment |
| Data collection planning | Feasibility study | Operating equipment |
| Data communication planning | Justification study and identification of benefits | File handling |
| Organization | | File library control |
| Management development planning | Identifying project controller | Output control |
| Specialist development planning | Resource planning | Computer operating management control and measurement system |
| Recruitment | Identifying project teams | |
| Training | Systems analysis | Data preparation management control and measurement system |
| Justification methods | Systems design | |
| Analysis, design, and programming methods | Systems requirements specification | Correction of program failures |
| Accounting and transfer-charging methods | Computer system design | Program efficiency improvement |
| Operating and maintenance methods | Computer system specification | |
| Management control systems | Programming | |
| Project planning methods | Module testing | |
| Language projection | Program and package construction | |
| Software projection | Package testing | |
| | Construction of test data | |
| | System testing | |
| | Operational testing | |

**Figure 3.9**

| Planning | Project development | Operating |
|---|---|---|
| | Equipment (acceptance) testing | |
| | Software testing | |
| | Project review with users | |
| | Project review with programmers | |
| | Project review with operating department | |
| | File data preparation | |
| | File conversion | |
| | Implementation | |

**Figure 3.9** (contd)

## 2. Identify key tasks contributing to departmental objectives

Remember that an objective is a statement of an important achievement *which will require planning effort* if it is to be attained. Objectives are improvement targets, and we must take special action, therefore, if we are to meet them. The computer department action plan should analyze the key tasks that need to be performed in order to achieve the overall objectives—and also who is responsible for performing them.

▶ The computer department referred to in 1 above completed its action plan using one of these further forms for each objective:

| Objective: Expected benefit: | | |
|---|---|---|
| Action required | By whom | By when |
| — | | |
| — | | |
| — | | |
| Action coordinator: | | |

**Figure 3.10**

This process of "breaking down" what the department is trying to achieve into separate tasks and objectives for the computer staff involves careful and detailed analysis. Three examples follow: each illustrates a different technique.

▶ **Case A**

This company found it helpful to construct a hierarchy of objectives. At corporate level, a part of the hierarchy can be seen in Figure 3.11.

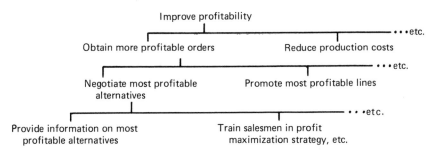

**Figure 3.11**

The "provision of information" objective was given to the computer department. They, in turn, constructed a further hierarchy, part of which is shown in Figure 3.12.

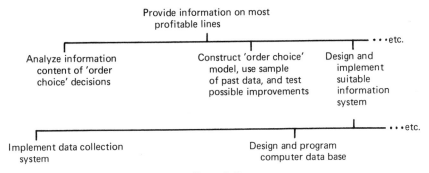

**Figure 3.12**

Note that these are not yet objectives in the MBO sense since they are not measured. The hierarchy is only a tool to aid analysis. Such hierarchies should be "pushed down" to the point where *someone has to take action*.

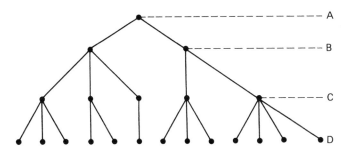

**Figure 3.13**

Some corporations describe their hierarchies as "end/means pyramids." Suppose we had a hierarchy consisting of four levels of objectives as in Figure 3.13. Objective A is our end. The means of achieving this end are the objectives described at level B. These means become, in turn, the ends of the next level down; i.e., the objectives at level B become the ends achieved by the means described at level C, and so on.

► **Case B**

The computer department of the financial institution that we referred to earlier when we gave examples of key areas, subsequently took each of these key areas and analyzed what key tasks would be needed to perform each one. They produced an analysis (Figure 3.14) for key area no. 1.

| No. | Key result areas | Key tasks |
|-----|-----------------|-----------|
| 1. | Achievement of benefits from use of Management Services Department services | 1. To identify (and agree with general managers on) the scope for the extension of the level and range of services provided. |
| | | 2. To identify user managers' need for services, and assist line managers to set priorities in terms of profit, cost, and customer service benefits. |
| | | 3. To develop and provide services which satisfy the needs of the user in terms of quality, level, cost, and time scale. |
| | | 4. To develop an awareness among staff at all levels of the services available, and promote their effective use. |
| | | 5. To analyze training needs of users, potential users, managers, and staff, and assist in their training. |
| | | 6. To maintain effective liaison with head office departments, in order to assist users in the implementation of systems and the achievement, evaluation, and consolidation of benefits. |
| | | 7. To develop and implement procedures for project audit. |
| | | 8. To prepare and maintain annual and five-year plans. |
| | | 9. To assist the chief accountant in the administration of policy for transfer charging, by the development and maintenance of an equitable system for management services costs. |

**Figure 3.14**   Key task analysis

► **Case C**

Another computer department used a results influence chart (Figure 3.15)

| | Administration | Systems development | Planning and research | Implementation | Operations |
|---|---|---|---|---|---|
| Functional purposes | To provide the department with human resources to enable its objectives to be met, and to develop and maintain administrative and training services to meet the needs of those resources. In addition, to maintain accounting information to enable management to monitor and control costs in relation to the department's work. | To develop computer-based systems in accordance with feasibility studies. To develop noncomputer systems. To implement and maintain clerical productivity measurement. | etc. | etc. | etc. |
| Departmental purposes | To continue development and maintenance of a management accounting system, and assist in the interpretation of results. To undertake transfer charging. To contribute to feasibility studies. To examine nontechnical contracts. | To contribute to feasibility studies. To design predetermined automated systems and their associated job structures. To write and document progress. To install clerical productivity measurement methods. To design and implement clerical procedures. To advise on selection of office and cash-handling equipment. | | | |

To design, implement, and operate systems (manual, mechanized, or automated as appropriate) to meet company's objectives, including the organization of work and assistance in the establishment of job structures within the user areas to achieve efficient management and operation of those systems. To: etc.

**Figure 3.15**

to analyze the important tasks to be undertaken. The chart took the form of a matrix. Along one axis they listed all the functions. Down the other they listed the various major purposes of the department. At the intersection they analyzed the contribution made by each function to each departmental purpose.

The results influence chart (or matrix analysis, as it is sometimes called) is a commonly used tool in MBO studies. The example in Figure 3.15 analyzed the influence which each function had on departmental purposes. But other analyses are, of course, possible. The matrix can be stated in the following general form:

|  | People (or positions, groups, etc.) |
|---|---|
| Activities (or purposes, key areas, departmental objectives, etc.) | The influence each person has on each activity (key tasks, or nature of this influence, i.e., responsible for it, advisory, provides information, etc.) |

**Figure 3.16**

## 3. Analyze key tasks with the individuals concerned

The point of the detailed analysis of the department is that we can subsequently analyze how each individual person *really* contributes to the overall objective.

▶ A large public utility, having three computer centers, included cost containment as one of its key areas. The annual cost of EDP (including equipment, staff, data preparation, etc.) was more than $21 million. They set the departmental objective as reducing annual costs by 2 per cent in 18 months. They then embarked on a key task analysis with each individual, without first analyzing what decisions and activities really influenced the achievement of this overall objective. Each computer center had its own manager, and the senior management looked to these three men to achieve the cost reduction required.

When the MBO advisers got down to analyzing with the computer center managers what their jobs entailed, it was found that these computer center managers had hardly any influence on the costs of the department. The computers were bought as a result of justification studies in which the managers played no part. The centers were staffed in accordance with standards prepared by the Personnel function. Rates of pay were laid down by Personnel. It was corporate policy that they occupied certain existing buildings, and the charge for these was calculated by the central administration department. The time taken to run programs was governed largely by the systems and programs given to them by the project development department. In fact, the only cost the managers controlled amounted to some $33,600 overtime occasioned by the degree of efficiency of run scheduling and computer operating.

The three managers were the highest paid in the department, and senior management became immediately concerned that they were employing highly paid staff in positions which apparently carried little responsibility. Furthermore, they began to doubt whether the department would be able to reduce its costs and meet its objectives. Somewhat belatedly, they drew up a results influence chart which then enabled them to make a realistic plan for cost reduction. This analysis showed that equipment justification, project justification, project control, and systems design were the tasks to concentrate on. It showed them that project leaders held the most important positions, and they made appropriate changes in the caliber and salaries of these men. The analysis also showed that the computer center managers held, in reality, highly responsible jobs—in much the same way that airline pilots have heavy responsibilities. Neither is responsible for the čost of the equipment and staff, but each has the care of these high investments handed over to him.

At this stage, we begin the work of preparing results guides for each senior member of the computer department. A results guide usually contains five columns, as in Figure 3.17.

| Key area | Key tasks | Objectives (or performance standard) | Improvement plan (or action plan) | Control data |
|----------|-----------|--------------------------------------|-----------------------------------|--------------|
|          |           |                                      |                                   |              |

**Figure 3.17**

The results guide will also have a cover sheet showing the items given in Figure 3.18.

Job_____     Job holder_____
Main purpose of job:

Position in organization:
Scope of job:
Limit of authority:

Date_____

**Figure 3.18**

Typically, results guides are prepared for computer managers and staff down to the level of senior analysts and senior programmers, senior computer operators, control and data preparation supervisors—in fact, all people who have responsibility for the work of others, together with any technical specialists whose work has an important influence on the results of the department, e.g., software specialists, program auditors, and so on.

Each person is usually assisted by the adviser (also known as a "change agent") in the preparation of his results guide. There are usually two principal interview sessions. The first interview is between the job holder and the adviser, after which the job holder will be able to prepare the first draft of his results guide. The second interview is a three-man interview with the job holder, his superior, and the adviser, prior to which the superior will receive a copy of the drafts which have been prepared. The aim of this session is to end up with the settling on a results guide agreed between the job holder and his superior.

The first thing to do is to divide the job into its main areas and list these (the key areas column). Then, examining each one in turn, ask if there is a key task in that area, i.e., a task which, if done well, will contribute toward the achievement of departmental objectives; or, if not given sufficient attention, will endanger their achievement. It is recognized that most things which are done have little impact upon results; there are many jobs which are necessary but which consist of routine or administrative chores. The aim is to isolate that minority of tasks which has a significant effect.

▶ The chief programmer in one installation included in his list of key areas "Investigating technical feasibility." During justification and feasibility studies, he spent a lot of time calculating file size, input and output volumes, memory usage, and run timings based on the information given him by the systems analyst. After some consideration, however, he did not include any of these among his key tasks. Previous estimates had always proved to be

| Key areas | Key tasks | Objectives |
|---|---|---|
| 1. Investigating technical feasibility | 1.1 To calculate final computer workload by estimating for unspecified data volumes and programs at initial survey stage. | |
| | 1.2 etc. | |

**Figure 3.19**

too low, sometimes by factors of two or three. He concluded that his first key task in this area was to make the right allowance for data volumes, operations, and program runs—which cannot be envisaged at the time of the initial studies. His results guide included the items shown in Figure 3.19.

A job holder may identify two or three key tasks in one area; in another area he may decide that he has no truly key tasks at all. When each area has been examined in turn there will probably be a draft containing:

Four to six key areas
Eight to twelve key tasks

## 4. Set objectives and action plans

This step, which involves trying to measure the effect of our efforts, is found by many to be one of the most difficult.

"Everybody talks about the quality of programs," said one chief programmer, "and I have to admit high quality is important—I dare not look at some of the early ones we wrote here. But how can you *measure* the quality of a program?"

Despite this difficulty, measurement is an essential part of the approach to improved computer efficiency. People respond to the challenge of a clear objective, and enjoy the satisfaction of achieving it, but if we do not measure what we set out to achieve, how will we know when we get there? How will we know when we have written a *high-quality* program? If we find it difficult to measure our objectives, we can, in fact, be pleased: it shows that we are thinking about the effect of our work more deeply than before. We are beginning to analyze what its real contribution is.

Having identified a key task—e.g., to improve the quality of programming—it is helpful when trying to set objectives to ask the question: "What will improve if I do this task well?" If the answer is "nothing," then clearly we must challenge whether this is a key task. When we have identified one or more things which would get better as a result, we should then ask: "By how much?" This process should not only identify the improvement areas, but also suggest to us the unit of measure to apply.

▶ An MBO adviser took this approach with the chief programmer referred to earlier, and together they posed the question, "What will improve if we achieve high-quality programs?" Fairly quickly, they produced three possible objectives:

(a) The time spent correcting faults in programs, once they become operational, should fall. (This was especially troublesome during the first six to twelve months; a large number of their programs got off to a bumpy start.)

(b) The time spent in changing programs to accommodate users' new requirements should fall. (It was found easier to rewrite many of the existing programs than to change them.)

(c) The running time on the computer should fall.

They then asked, "By how much?" in each of the three cases—and added the following objectives (Figure 3.20) to the chief programmer's results guide.

| Key areas | Key tasks | Objectives | Action plan | Control data |
|---|---|---|---|---|
| Programmer productivity | To improve the quality of programs | (a) To reduce reruns due to program faults to four hours per month by January 1. | | |
| | | (b) To reduce program correction time to 12 man-hours per week by January 1. | | |
| | | (c) To reduce average delay in implementing user changes to 9 weeks, without increasing staff, by July 1. | | |
| | | (d) To reduce run time of hospital remittance and cost analysis package to 6 hours 45 minutes per week by August 6. | | |

**Figure 3.20**

At first sight, the setting of objectives may appear a simple exercise: after all, if each man is *already* clear about the important results he has to achieve, the standards he should adhere to, and the information he needs to tell him how he is getting on, the analysis will take little time and be comparatively unrewarding. In practice, however, most managers—not just those of the computer department—are unclear about these critical issues. For example:

▶ When Dr. N. F. Maier and Dr. L. R. Hoffmann, of the University of Michigan, conducted detailed interviews with 222 managerial "pairs," as part of a study of differences in job perception between boss and subordinate, only 8.1 per cent showed almost complete agreement. Regarding obstacles in the way of effective subordinate performance, there was almost complete disagreement in 38.6 per cent of the pairs.

▶ In an engineering firm, it is reported that ". . . the stated most important objective in the eyes of top management was an improvement in the poor delivery situation. Yet, during a survey of individual priorities, only 1 out of 86 in the production department saw this as his responsibility, and many had no regular information on deliveries available to them".

▶ In a computer survey made in a building supplies firm, we found the following situation. The objective for the computer as perceived by senior management varied from:

To give me more information about the business—president.

To reduce the number of order processing clerks—chief accountant.

To reduce inventory levels—chief buyer.

To eliminate errors in invoices and improve deliveries—sales director.

Nowhere were these objectives written down. It seemed that the computer was to be all things to all men, and that these beliefs were formed during "pairs" discussions between each of these directors and a member of the original justification team.

The following case study provides an interesting example of the confusion that can arise if boss and subordinate do not think through their objectives together.

▶ The management services director of a large food and confectionery manufacturer had the objective of reducing computer processing costs. He had communicated this to his senior computer staff at a meeting in his office, which had ended with the injunction that "We must all do what we can to keep costs as low as possible." About six months later, the computer manager—who was responsible for the day to day running of the computer —showed the management services director an analysis of computer time for the last year, and pointed out that since the campaign to reduce costs had started he had been able to reduce nonproductive computer time from 28 to 12 per cent. His director congratulated him. Thereafter, the productive and nonproductive computer times were published weekly, and it was generally accepted to be a good thing to keep the productive time high.

A year later, as part of a general MBO exercise in the company, the MBO adviser analyzed the key area "cost containment" with the computer manager. The adviser found that productive time was "all the time that users paid for." Nonproductive time was the time not charged to users, e.g., idle time, machine maintenance, program testing, etc. Extra running time on the computer, due to incorrect data and misoperating, was charged to the user, and was therefore "productive time."

Following this analysis, they concluded that in order to contain costs, the computer manager's objectives should in fact be reversed. He should maximize his nonproductive time, *not* his productive time. He should seek to use the machine as little as possible, consistent with producing the output required by the users. This change in the perception of his objective led later to improvements in operating efficiency, improvements in programs (made to reduce run time), and improvements in the quality of data supplied by the users. It enabled them to take on order processing and invoicing for two further factories without purchasing a new computer that had already been chosen for this work.

At this stage it is important that we distinguish the two different management problems:

The management of the day to day situation.

The management of projects.

The former is concerned with management where the major factors in the situation continue largely unchanged, e.g., the computer is operated every day, the major computer jobs repeat at regular intervals, the organization structure and the staff involved stay the same for long periods. And when changes do take place, they build on the existing computer jobs and the existing organization. There are rarely *completely* fresh situations to handle. It follows from all this, therefore, that the management of the day to day situation is not normally carried out in an "objectives" environment. Left to itself, the atmosphere is likely to be that of "trying to cope with the existing situation." The approach of regularly trying to achieve specific and challenging improvements—in short, of managing by objectives—has to be introduced artificially. The situation itself does not provide them.

Contrast this with the management of projects. Projects are specifically set up to deal with "once only" problems. Very little, if anything, is repetitive in the situation. Unique problems are constantly arising, e.g., the analysis and design of a new inventory control system, the reorganization of the inventory department, the writing of the new computer programs involved, etc. The people involved in the project frequently are brought together for the first time. A new team is formed for the purpose of the project, and this team is outside the established organization structure and management hierarchy. We can see, therefore, that project management takes place naturally in an "objectives" environment. The whole exercise is mounted to achieve a new objective. The efforts of all concerned are naturally, and without artificial stimulus, directed toward its achievement.

The distinction between these two forms of management is particularly important in computer departments, since systems development projects form a major part of the work they carry out. We have already dealt with the setting of objectives in the day to day situation. What are the differences when objectives are set for project management? Basically, we shall find it an easier exercise, since this work already takes place in an "objectives" environment. But there are three important points to watch:

The staff members form a "temporary group" outside the management hierarchy.

The objectives are frequently wrongly cast.

Special review techniques are required.

We will deal with the first two of these now. The special review techniques are considered at the end of Part 3, when we deal with the review of objectives, key areas, performance, etc., as a whole.

## Project staff

The things to watch in this connection are firstly that, since project staff are, for the purpose of their project work, outside the day to day management situation, they will also be outside any MBO system introduced for day to day management. Time and again, we have found MBO introduced into the computer department, covering every manager and senior person in it, and coping admirably with the continuing situation. These systems can only deal with projects as a generality, e.g., "to finish all projects on time," "to meet estimated computer run times in all projects," etc. They do nothing whatever for any *specific* project. A particular project can only be dealt with by treating it separately from MBO in the department, developing its own special hierarchy of objectives, identifying the key tasks for each project member, and then preparing results guides for each person involved in the project.

To distinguish these exercises from the overall departmental MBO system, we have found one or two installations that prepared two separate sets of documents: "project result guides" and "result guides." In this connection, we should notice that the same person may have both project objectives (as a member of a project team) and improvement objectives covering the day to day situation in his capacity as a manager. For example, the chief programmer may hold objectives to:

Design the inventory control package by March 16—*project objective.*

Reduce the nonproductive programming time to 7 per cent by December 31 —*improvement objective.*

The second aspect, regarding project staff, concerns the design of objectives to suit individuals. The MBO style of management calls for each person to develop his own objective in conjunction with his boss. There will be a blend of what the department wants to achieve and what the individual feels he can (and wants to) contribute. Objectives are personal in this sense. It is, therefore, fundamental to the approach that people do not leave their jobs until their objectives have been achieved. Of course, circumstances arise in which this ideal cannot be achieved! But it is of particular importance in the project environment—which is, by nature, a temporary group, and where we have found a tendency in many installations for people to join and leave the group during the life of the project.

▶ An engineering firm had an average of five computer development projects going on at any given time. Project leaders were carefully chosen for their personal qualities as well as their technical skills and company knowledge. By definition, therefore, they were people who were "going places" and ultimately destined for senior positions in the firm. Openings for their talents arose from time to time in the corporation, and the project leaders themselves were keen to get on. It became the rule rather than the exception for leading a project to be a steppingstone to a senior job; if a project leader demonstrated good qualities, he would be promoted off the project *before* it was completed.

At this stage, projects which had previously been going well deteriorated, and discussions about the project objectives, terms of reference, and the basic strategy adopted always took place. In the end, the corporation recognized that it was unrealistic for a new project leader to accept objectives and action plans developed and agreed in his absence. Only through involvement in the setting of the original objectives could they make plans which suited the style and abilities of the project leader, and achieve the personal commitment required. Accordingly, they formulated a new policy that "the only way off a project was for the project member concerned to have met his objectives." In the case of project leaders, this meant that the only way off the project was to finish it!

WRONGLY CAST OBJECTIVES

While project management is well used to setting objectives and planning and controlling work to meet them, the objectives accepted by computer project teams are frequently misplaced. We have found that most project leaders, when asked what their objectives are, reply, "To get this project going by X date." Computer projects are commonly geared to target dates; sometimes, but rarely, objectives are defined for the computer system itself—e.g., to produce statements for 40,000 accounts by the first Tuesday of every month. Hardly ever does the project leader hold objectives for getting any company benefit from the computer system. Frequently, when such "benefit" objectives are defined they are misconceived and fall into the "clerical savings" category—which, as we saw in Part 2, completely misses the point of automation.

▶ The manager of a large computer department serving a group of firms manufacturing metal pipes and fittings and other metal products strongly resisted the general allegation that most companies were disappointed with their computers. He cited the case of his own department, in which the computer projects had been "completely satisfactory." When asked what benefits had been achieved, however, he replied, "We don't look at it that way." Further discussions showed that what he meant by "satisfactory" was that technically the projects had completely fulfilled their requirements. The stock control programs did maintain stock records and produce reorder quantities, the payroll produced accurate pay slips, and so on. After some thought he then said, "We've gotten a lot out of these systems—production has found that they've been able to reduce work in progress from 7,000 tons of copper to 2,000 tons. Nobody believed the work schedules before, and they used to requisition materials and start manufacture far too early, to give themselves safety margins. The computer information has meant they can work to much finer limits."

After more thought he said, "And customer service has improved no end. Mr. Richards told me last week they would have been out of business if they had not been able to quote prices and delivery within 24 hours this last year. . . ."

This story illustrates two important points. Satisfactory and unsatisfactory computer jobs are considered by many people to be those jobs which work on the computer and those that do not. Secondly, the benefits to the company—important though they may be in some cases—are frequently not identified as objectives for the project at its commencement. They may or may not arise later, and are certainly not in the forefront of the computer project leader's mind.

▶ The automobile components corporation we described earlier, which implemented an entirely satisfactory inventory control computer system and achieved no benefits because no one in the company had the job or objective of reducing stocks, decided to remedy this situation for future projects. They divided project objectives into four categories.

*Time objectives:* the date the project is to be operational.

*Cost objectives:* the project budget.

*Systems objectives:* the outputs the system is to produce, using specified inputs.

*Improvement objectives:* the benefit the company is to aim for as a result of the system.

For each project, they drew up a hierarchy of objectives for each of these categories, for example:

*Time:* the time by which each project activity should be completed.

*Cost:* a breakdown of the budget for each project activity.

*System:* the technical accomplishment required from each project activity if the overall systems objective is to be achieved—e.g., program A4 to progress 2,000 orders per hour; disk access routines to achieve 4 per second; a maximum of three orders per 1,000 to require manual processing; less than one order per 500 to be rejected by data preparation, etc.

*Improvement:* the supporting improvements necessary if the overall improvement is to be achieved—e.g., representatives to get orders in by 11:00 next morning; new racking system to cope with stock picking and color matching in one operation; sales manager to forecast sales by product group instead of overall sale; nonstandard orders to be refused in future; containers to be chargeable; customers exceeding credit limit to be refused further orders, etc.

Lastly, the achievement of every subobjective in each of these four categories was made the personal responsibility of someone.

We regard the division of project objectives into these four categories to be of fundamental importance. Of course, the achievement of *improvement* objectives does not have to be the responsibility of the project leader; unless he is given line authority in the user's department, he will be powerless to achieve them. The installation just described, in fact, agreed the improvement objectives with the user, and he accepted responsibility for their achievement. An alternative is to have the user be the project leader. The key points are:

Every project should have the improvement objectives defined at the start.

These objectives should be broken down into a hierarchy of necessary subobjectives, with the people who are in a position to achieve them, who then accept them as their personal objectives.

## IMPROVEMENT PLANS

We earlier defined an objective as a target which *requires planning effort for its achievement.* It is something which we are not at present achieving and which, unless we take some special action and change the way we are going about things, we shall not achieve in future. It is no use setting an objective and then sitting back and expecting it to be fulfilled.

Having set an objective, we must next make a plan to achieve it. A column is provided in the results guide to describe this action plan. An action plan may take any suitable form, however: for example, a Gantt chart or a network is a convenient way to express action plans. Where appropriate, such detailed plans supplement the brief description given in the results guide itself.

In preparing action plans, it is helpful to study the measured objective, and then to ask such questions as:

Why aren't we achieving this at present?

Do I or my staff need special training?

Should we change our methods?

What other people in the department or in the firm need to make changes if I am to achieve this objective?

Did we ever achieve this objective? If so, what has changed since then?

The chief programmer's results guide referred to earlier contained the action plans below (Figure 3.21).

| Objectives | Action plan | Control data |
|---|---|---|
| 1 To reduce reruns due to program faults to four hours per month by January 1. | To provide internal training course on fault diagnosis. | |
| 2. To reduce "program correction" time to 12 man-hours per week by January 1. | To reduce size of all modules to 35 source instructions maximum on all future projects. To rewrite B.17 and B.19 in modular construction. | |
| 3. To reduce average delay in implementing user changes to 9 weeks (without increasing staff) by July 1. | | |
| 4. To reduce run time of hospital remittances and cost analysis package to 6 hours 45 minutes each week by August 6. | To rewrite data, validate and file update routines employing strategy shown on attached flowchart. | |

**Figure 3.21**

Action plans can frequently have a fundamental effect on the methods employed in the department:

▶ A large steel corporation had been one of the pioneers of computer data processing. In 1970 they had six major projects in progress and, in addition to project leaders on each project, employed a projects controller to manage projects generally. They had a long record of successful technical accomplishment behind them, but despite this, they experienced problems of cost and time escalation on all their projects. They identified project control as a key area. During MBO sessions with the projects controller, his key tasks and objectives were set, some of which are shown in Figure 3.22.

| Key task | → | With the result that | → | Objectives |
|----------|---|---------------------|---|------------|
| To improve project estimating and control techniques | | | | 1. All further projects meet time and cost targets settled on with users at feasibility stage or at a subsequent user review meeting |
| | | | | 2. All present projects hold user review meetings within the next four months to settle on firm time and cost targets |

**Figure 3.22**

When the project controller and the MBO adviser came to prepare action plans to achieve the objective, they first analyzed the present projects. They found:

1. The average length of these six current projects was 2.8 years to date (and still continuing).
2. Two of the current projects were over five years old.

The apparently never-ending nature of the projects inevitably led to escalation beyond the original project objectives, to changes in the project team, and to poor control. Further investigation showed that "user changes" arose with such regularity in the programs produced by the projects that, although four of the current projects had long since gotten their initial programs operational, they seemed to have become engaged in a full-time program maintenance operation. It was decided that since maintenance of this type was a *continuing* activity, it was unsuitable for a project style of management. The project controller's action plans therefore included:

1. A stage in all projects was defined at which the systems development objectives become "frozen."
2. The responsibility for changes in programs (necessitated by subsequent changes in the "frozen objectives") was removed from the project leader and passed to a new maintenance section that employed a line management rather than a project management approach and that reported to the operations manager.

The example shows that one man's action plans can frequently involve other people. For this reason, a number of computer departments distinguish two types of plans:

Individual action plans
Group action plans

► A corporation employing four computer centers, run by a central management services department, had originally organized the department into two functions, planning and data processing, as shown in Figure 3.23.

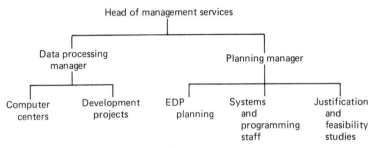

**Figure 3.23**

Analyzing the key area "costs," they had difficulty in providing action plans for any one individual which would have a major effect on costs. Computer center managers could do little on their own, since the planners had determined their equipment for them. The planners could not reduce the anticipated equipment requirements, since they could not influence the efficiency of systems development and computer operating—the main cause of the need for more equipment. Project leaders had little say concerning their staff or the terms of reference set during justification studies, and so on. It appeared that the whole department was involved in each individual cost saving activity, and accordingly a number of group action plans were formulated. This analysis led them to the view that their organizational structure made cost containment difficult. One of the most important group action plans, therefore, was to reorganize the department into two groups which reflected the two distinct cost centers, equipment and project development. This group action plan contained the proposed reorganization shown in Figure 3.24.

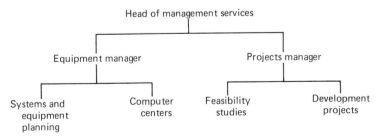

**Figure 3.24**

## 5. Set performance standards

A performance standard is a level of achievement which we wish to maintain. It does not, like an objective, state a measured improvement. Since we are trying to make the computer department more efficient, one may well remark that surely it is only improvements we are interested in. However, many firms have learned to their cost, that an effort to make improvements often brings with it a tendency to neglect important routine operations. These operations, which were previously running satisfactorily, deteriorate and the departmental efficiency declines, despite the achievement of the improvement objective.

> ▶ Two firms, each having a computer, were involved in a merger. Corporation A had a small third-generation computer producing monthly statements quite satisfactorily. The other, corporation B, had recently installed a large fourth-generation machine with some real-time facilities, and was in the process of implementing an order processing system with real-time stock interrogation. It was decided to process the statements for both companies on the third-generation machine. Hardly any program changes were required, since it was decided that corporation B should adopt the same accounting system as A. It was also decided that all the processing, invoicing, and stock interrogations for both companies should be done on the newer, fourth-generation machine. This represented a far greater degree of system sophistication for corporation A than it had been planning. The excitement and challenge of this new project captured their interest. The management assigned most of the computer staff to it, and settled on objectives with them. However, morale dropped among the staff left to work with the old machine, and program maintenance almost ceased. Management showed no interest in the performance standards achieved by this department, despite the fact that they now had double the number of statements to produce. If the previous performance standards had been maintained, this extra load could have been processed in the three shifts allowed for the old computer. Following the lack of management attention, however, efficiency fell, and a fourth, weekend shift had to be instituted. After two months, the staff refused to continue working the weekend shift, and a crisis developed in the company concerning its customer accounts—a crisis which, it was later estimated, cost over $144,000 in lost postings and statements.

Performance standards for one chief operator are shown in Figure 3.25.

While a chief operator will certainly have some objectives in his results guide, all the goals extracted below represent performance standards—targets which it is important to maintain *in addition* to getting improvements in other areas. The results guide will not, of course, contain any

| Key area | Key task | Objectives or performance standards | Action plans | Control data |
|---|---|---|---|---|
| 1. Operating efficiency | 1.1. To meet monthly output schedules | 1.1.1. Fourth day statements | | |
| | | 1.1.2. Eighth day, monthly sales statistics | | |
| | | 1.1.3. Thirteenth day, profit and loss statement | | |
| | 1.2. To minimize reruns | 1.2.1. Two hours maximum per month | | |

**Figure 3.25** Results guide.

action plans opposite performance standards, since they are already being achieved.

As further examples, it may be helpful to look at the list of actual objectives and performance standards, taken from a number of different installations, that is shown in Figure 3.26. The variety of these examples illustrates that there can be no "general" objectives or performance standards that can be adopted, ready made, by a computer department.

| Key areas | Key tasks | Who | Objectives/ performance standards |
|---|---|---|---|
| Examination of use made of outputs | To analyze the circulation list for all sales reports. | Systems manager | To obtain a ranked appraisal for each report from each recipient by October 2. |
| Achievement of targets | To redesign credit control system to reduce the credit period. | Systems manager | To obtain user's agreement, by January 14, that the revised system will reduce average age of accounts receivable to 2.4 months. |
| | To reduce run time of the customer file updating program. | Chief programmer | To reduce the run time from 160 to 35 minutes. |
| | To reduce the input error rate on work order tickets. | Operations manager | To achieve 2 per cent record rejection by next quarter. |

**Figure 3.26**

| Key areas | Key tasks | Who | Objectives/ performance standards |
|---|---|---|---|
| Return on investment | To identify the corporate benefits that have been made possible by computer operations. | Data processing manager | To settle on a list with users by October 1. |
| Target planning | To settle on time and cost targets with users. | Data processing manager | To settle on targets by the end of Septermber. |
| Meeting changed requirements | To schedule planned systems revisions. | Data processing manager | To get revisions finished on time. |
| Machine utilization | To minimize the level of program testing time. | Chief programmer | To reduce trials to 1.8 per development module and 1.2 per module amendment by June 6. |
| Program efficiency | To reduce the processing time of the daily run customer accounts. | Chief programmer | To increase the accounts file processing speed to within 65 per cent of the nominal tape speed by end of October. |
| Program breakdown | To rewrite the error routine modules for AF162. | Chief programmer | No further program stoppages on AF162 after April 6. |
| Manpower allocation | To make correct allowances for priority maintenance in development planning schedules. | Chief programmer | To remove, for next quarter, slippage in development work programming schedules caused by priority maintenance. |
| Morale | To maintain programmers' enthusiasm after the project is completed. | Chief programmer | To reduce programmers' turnover from 32 to 15 per cent next year. |
| Recruitment | To attract the right caliber of responses to advertisements for programmers. | Personnel officer | To improve success rate to three or more offers per advertisement, maintaining our 8 per cent "satisfactory" standard. |
| Effectiveness of communication | To maintain the data dictionary. | Systems analyst | No systems errors due to ambiguity over item descriptions during the next year. |
| Control of subcontractors | To avoid cost escalation. | Data processing manager | To obtain a fixed price quotation from all subcontractors in the future. |

**Figure 3.26** (contd)

| Key areas | Key tasks | Who | Objectives/ performance standards |
|-----------|-----------|-----|-----------------------------------|
| Project testing | To predict test data results. | Chief programmer | No test data to be submitted for computer processing without senior programmer's initials on predicted outputs. |
| Project development costs | To control program development costs. | Programming manager | To reduce program development costs to 22¢ per developed instruction for the next accounting period. |
| | | | To reduce nonproductive ratio to 38 per cent by June 1. |
| | | | To improve output to 5.2 tested source instructions per hour by June 1. |
| | | | To reduce trials to 13 minutes per 100 instructions, etc., by April 1. |
| Resource allocation | To estimate key-punch time for next quarter. | Programming manager | To estimate data preparation load for INPROD project within 15 per cent accuracy of actual for each week of the project by March 14. |
| Specification of requirements | To specify files and record sizes for customer accounting and stock control. | Chief programmer | To prepare estimated file volumes within 15 per cent of actual by February 15. |
| | To produce a specification of the Leeds production control job. | Systems manager | All manufacturers to accept specification with no further queries by April 10. |
| Identifying suppliers | To prepare a short list of existing equipment that is to be replaced. | Data processing manager | To submit list to the divisional director by August 6. |
| | To subcontract a "spare parts scheduling" program package. | Chief programmer | To obtain three competitive quotations for comparison at the next planning committee meeting. |

**Figure 3.26** (contd)

| Key areas | Key tasks | Who | Objectives/ performance standards |
|---|---|---|---|
| Assessing proposals | To simulate actual run times on order processing, for performance comparison of the proposed equipment by various manufacturers. | Chief programmer | To prepare programs by March 8.<br><br>To estimate run times per 1,000 orders to within 12 per cent of actual for next proposal. |
| Work scheduling | To prepare weekly timetable of priorities for nonroutine tasks, and daily revisions where necessary. | Data processing manager | To prepare timetable by 9:45 a.m. Monday, revisions daily by 9:45 a.m. |
| | To identify priorities for program complications and trials weekly, and make daily revisions where necessary. | Chief programmer | To identify priorities by 9:45 a.m. Monday, revisions daily by 9:45 a.m. |
| | To prepare daily 24-hour work schedule from 10:30 a.m. | Operations manager | To circulate work schedule to chief operator, librarian, and shift leaders by 10:15 a.m. daily. |
| User service | To hold meetings with user department representatives on errors/deadlines performance. | Data processing manager | To hold one meeting per user department per month. |
| | To reduce key-punch errors. | Operations manager | To reduce errors to 1 per cent of documents by end of year (= 0.1 per cent of cards). |
| | To eliminate errors in library records. | Librarian | To issue no wrong tapes in next three months. |
| Machine utilization | To minimize lost time on computer. | Operations manager | To ensure that 97 per cent of uptime is devoted to productive operating during third quarter. |
| | To devise amended routing system such that orders will reach department half-day earlier than now. | Chief systems analyst | To submit report by November 1. |
| | To eliminate unnecessary compilation runs. | Chief programmer | To have all data for program compilation ready for punching by 4 p.m. To reduce failures by 50 per cent during quarter ending October 31. |

**Figure 3.26** (contd)

| Key areas | Key tasks | Who | Objectives/ performance standards |
|---|---|---|---|
| Supplies provisioning | To introduce stationery wastage report. | Data processing manager | To complete report by July 31. |
| | To reduce stocks of cards to safe limits consistent with obtaining most favorable prices. | Operations manager | To negotiate call-off contracts for yearly requirements by March 31. |
| Operating costs | To reduce running time of order processing package. | Chief programmer | To modify pricing program to save 10 per cent of time by March 31. |
| | To reduce running time of order processing package. | Chief systems analyst | To specify system for automatic selection of discount to avoid manual look-up and recording by February 28. |
| | To reduce running time of order processing package. | Chief operator | To "string" programs for invoicing package and achieve 20 per cent improvement in multi-program running of programs 270 and 271 with program 275 by April 22. |
| Program breakdown | To institute early warning system of program breakdowns causing delays on delivery note package. | Data processing manager | To have dispatch manager at warehouse advised within 10 minutes, on every occasion during quarter, of all breakdowns over 60 minutes. |
| | To reduce delays caused by program breakdown. | Chief programmer | To reduce lost time by six hours during quarter ending September 30. |
| Machine maintenance | To prepare weekly maintenance schedules for computer and punches. | Operations manager | To complete schedules by 12:00 p.m. each Friday. |
| | To maintain a log of faults for each item of equipment. | Chief operator | To have log ready for presenting to data processing manager by 11:00 a.m. each Monday |
| Feasibility | To prepare a systems specification for presentation to selected computer manufacturers. | Systems manager | To have specification completed by October 1, so that manufacturers can prepare bids by December 20. |

**Figure 3.26** (contd)

| Key areas | Key tasks | Who | Objectives/ performance standards |
|-----------|-----------|-----|-----------------------------------|
| Department requirements | To produce a list of staff requirements in each grade to carry out the planned work during the next six months. | Systems manager | To prepare plan by April 7 which enables us to meet agreed-on work deadlines. |
| | To determine the programming effort, in terms of time and resources, necessary to implement the proposed stock-recording system. | Programming manager | To estimate the programming cost for the project within 10 per cent of actual by April 1. |
| | To formulate and review the allocation of staff between sections, upon the introduction of "on-line" data input. | Operations manager | To produce report by December 1. |
| Return on investment | To sell space on computer facilities to outside organizations. | Data processing manager | To reduce the cost to the company of data processing by $24,000 per annum by the end of the year. |
| Assessment of future scope | To develop plans for introducing automatic reordering capacity into the stock-recording system. | Systems manager | To settle on plans with users by May 1. |

**Figure 3.26** (contd)

To be useful, such objectives and standards must be personal to the particular installation and the particular people involved. From the regular "installation audits" which Urwick Dynamics carries out for a number of clients, even apparently general performance standards concerning computer maintenance time, staff turnover, staff salaries, and data preparation key-punch errors have been found to differ widely—and with good reason.

## 6. Set up review information systems

The last column in the results guide (Figure 3.25) is labeled "Control data." In this column, we state the information source or sources which enable us to measure the extent to which we are achieving our objectives and performance standards. There are two major points to note. Firstly, it does no good whatsoever to take the trouble to define a measured objective as a goal if we do not have a way of measuring whether it is being achieved.

A chief programmer once told us this story: "We were all called in by the big man and given this 'cost reduction' pep talk. Our company gets these fads from time to time. And he said, 'Okay, what can each of you save?' And no one said anything, so he started asking each person specifically. Everyone was saying how much pressure there was on the resources they had and how they would need a lot of time to think about it. And when it got to me, I said quietly, but without any pause, 'I can save $67,000 on program development this year.' He was delighted. Frankly, there wasn't the slightest chance of his ever knowing what my costs were—no one knows when the programmers work for me and when they are doing user liaison—let alone what the split between development and and maintenance is!"

Secondly, in order to achieve objectives (i.e., to make an *improvement*), we shall probably have to do something new, or in a new way. It is unlikely that there is any existing information showing what performance this new thing will achieve. If there were, it is likely that someone would have done something about it before.

▶ A chief programmer set the following objective with each of his team leaders:

To reduce the size of all modules to 40 source instructions maximum on all future projects.

Having set this objective, a system had to be set up to measure module sizes. Before the chief programmer investigated the key area "Implementation of user changes" and perceived that changes were difficult to make because so much of each program was affected by even the simplest change, no one knew how big the modules being written actually were.

To design the control data, we should ask the question:

"How does the job holder know whether or not the performance level is being achieved?"

A man may be quite clear about his objectives and work conscientiously to achieve them. But factors outside his knowledge or authority—or both —may cause him to fall below the required level. Unless he knows this through adequate control information, he cannot take corrective action quickly and effectively. Self-control is the important goal here.

Controls may include documents such as budgets, weekly utilization reports, and so on; or formal and informal meetings and observations. Consider the computer manager. At its simplest, his level of performance might be: "To maintain productive time at 77 per cent of 'switched-on' time." This measure is too crude to give much assistance in improving performance, however. A breakdown of unproductive time into, say:

    Computer maintenance
    Program testing
    Reruns
    Idle time

each with a standard of performance, is certain to lead to investigations and the setting up of improvement plans. In the area of reruns, a further analysis by cause will be helpful. For example:

    Misoperation
    User error
    Program error
    Data control error

Experience shows that a lot of rerun time is often shown as productive time, especially if a program is rerun at the request of the user. The point of this measurement is to bring these things out into the open so that improvements can be made.

In the last analysis, the best measure of productive time is according to productivity. For example, to maintain a 77 per cent level of productive time is not necessarily a good thing. What did we achieve in that time? This achievement could be high or low depending on:

    The efficiency of operating
    The scheduling of the work
    The element of rerun in the work
    The configuration of equipment used
    The "shared" work (in time-sharing configurations)
    The strategy of the programming

A simple measure of output—e.g., the number of invoice lines produced—is a start, but productivity depends on the interrelationship of a number of factors, such as:

    Volume of output
    Type of output
    Volume of input
    Type of input
    Records updated
    File amendments, insertions, deletions
    Processing volume

Fortunately, the computer itself can determine the volume of these factors each time the program is run. Therefore the effect of the various factors can fairly easily be worked out, and once productive time is related to productivity, the way in which improvements can be obtained is highlighted.

Control information is important for human as well as planning reasons. A man's time and interest quite properly focus on the signals received from control information: if the pattern is misleading and misdirected, so will be the effort. As Drucker points out:

> . . . the measurement used determines what one pays attention to . . . it makes things visible and tangible. The things included in the measurement become relevant; the things omitted are out of sight and mind.

In our experience, it would be most unusual to analyze any job in the computer department and not find scope for improvement in the controls:

Need for greater simplicity
Different frequency
Too much information so that perception and discrimination are blocked
Historical information too late for helpful corrective action
Overpreoccupation with financial controls, and not enough concern for management information

The relevant part of the results guide for one computer operating manager, concerned with measuring the work actually accomplished by his computer is shown in Figure 3.27.

| Key area | Key task | Objective | Action plan | Control data |
|----------|----------|-----------|-------------|--------------|
| Cost control | To improve the efficiency of computer operating | To remove cost increases not justified by increased processing volume for next year | To introduce computer work measurement | 1. Shift operation<br>2. Time and work analysis sheet<br>3. Computer log<br>4. "Switched-on" analysis sheet<br>5. Work volumes from data preparation bonus sheets<br>6. EDP quarterly cost summary |

**Figure 3.27**

Merely to have each person in the computer department analyze and agree with his boss his tasks, standards, and controls would be major progress. But it is not enough. To stop at that point would be to imply that the present arrangements and expectations are basically satisfactory and all that is required is to clarify and communicate. The exciting and rewarding feature of preparing job results guides is that there is a constructive opportunity to challenge and seek improvement in every aspect of the job—starting with

> "Is that job really necessary at all?"

and going on to

> We always work to this standard of performance and no one complains. However, how does it compare with the best installations in Britain and the USA?
>
> This standard has impact on our customers (other departments), yet we made it without discussion with them.
>
> This job is clearly needed, but its organizational relationship with others in the department is confused.
>
> We preach the need for good information systems, yet within our own section of this computer department we do not have a good control pattern.

and so on.

This offers an opportunity to tap the capacity for creativity which is undoubtedly widespread in computer departments. Any results guide which does not contain half-a-dozen worthwhile ideas for change and improvement is automatically suspect.

## Task forces

We have seen that many improvement plans lead to the need for group action, not just individual action. The approach we have described, leading to the preparation of results guides for each senior person in the computer department, is largely geared to improving the performance of individuals. As part of the exercise, therefore, it is useful to set up task forces for studying areas in which group action is felt to be needed. These task forces will comprise about five or six people who have experience with, and knowledge of, the various problems arising in the area. The members should also represent the various functions involved. The purpose of the task force is to produce recommendations. These recommendations are then presented to top management, i.e., to the management level at which the actions proposed by the task force can be approved. Management discusses the findings with the task force, and action plans are established for the various people involved.

We discussed the role and composition of task forces at some length in Part 2. The task force we described there was formed specifically for the purpose of identifying business improvements in the key areas of the company made possible by automation. The task forces we are now discussing have a different role—that of studying important problems affecting the efficiency of the computer department. A number of these task forces may be set up. Very often, the important issues are already clearly known. In such cases a task force program can be drawn up during the preliminary study.

▶ One computer department identified the following seven subjects for study, to be completed during the first six months of the MBO exercise. They used different teams for each study, with members drawn from the computer department and from the rest of the company.

> Project management
> Staff productivity
> Computer equipment productivity
> Achievement of user benefits
> Audit of projects and installations
> Training of user managers and staff
> Preparation and use of five-year plan

The SWOT analysis approach, described earlier, is often found useful in task force work.

▶ A public utility, in analyzing the target for the key area "Meeting time and cost," recognized that project coordination was a major problem. They set up a task force to study this problem and make recommendations. The task force consisted of:

> A project controller
> A senior manager in a user department
> The cost accountant
> An outside consultant
> The head of data processing standards

Firstly, the task force completed a strengths, weaknesses, opportunities, and threats analysis as in Figure 3.28:

After further study, management produced recommendations in the form of action plans covering various headings such as:

> Authorizing systems changes
> Changing project leaders during projects
> Project cost control, etc.

| Strengths | Weaknesses | Opportunities | Threats |
|---|---|---|---|
| We appoint a full-time project controller for each project. | Project controller's authority is not universally accepted.<br><br>The formal communications and organization structure is inadequately defined.<br><br>Individual responsibilities are not formally specified.<br><br>Methods of planning control and coordination are not standard. | The recent development of systems and programming standards in the department. | The increasing program maintenance load, which makes it difficult to:<br><br>1. Get programmers full time on development projects.<br>2. Define the end of a project. |

**Figure 3.28**    SWOT analysis—project coordination.

| Summary | Action | By whom | Dates |
|---|---|---|---|
| There is a need to develop and implement the second phase of the management accounting system, already agreed to in principle by the planning committee, and covering an accounting system allocating costs to projects. | Develop and implement a project-oriented cost control system to include:<br>1. The establishment of the standard costs of using defined units of resource.<br>2. The preparation of budgets for projects:<br>  i. by stage and, where appropriate, by activity within stage;<br>  ii. by designated calendar period.<br>3. A system of reporting on the progress of a project so that control of costs can be exercised by all levels of management by activity, stage, or calendar period as appropriate.<br>4. A method of calculating costs and a standard format for the provision of cost data. | Cost accountant | Complete by end of July. |

**Figure 3.29**    Action plan—project cost control.

The plan concerning project cost control is shown in Figure 3.29. These plans were presented to the senior managers of the corporation at a half-day meeting, during which the plan, with certain revisions, was agreed. Overall, the task force met for five three-hour discussions, and each member put in a further two days' work outside meetings.

It is common during task force work for a paper to be produced which attempts to provide the corporation concerned with some fresh insight or understanding of the problem. The following extracts, taken from the work of task forces in five different organizations, provide interesting examples of this, each in an area of general interest.

► **Case A**

JUSTIFICATION STUDIES

This firm had a history of computer justification studies covering both the purchase of computer equipment and extra work on existing equipment. The results subsequently achieved had not been the measured benefits identified in the justification study—there was currently a view that "these benefits are not measurable anyway." A further proposal had been put forward for increased equipment costing $720,000 to be used in implementing a "management information system." The board members were hesitant about authorizing this purchase (together with the implementation and systems disruption costs) as "an act of faith," and a task force was set up to examine the problem.

The task force found that all justification studies in the past in this company had been:

1. Based on "clerical savings."
2. Prepared by service departments (accounts, computer department, etc.) and not by user departments.

They advanced the view that service departments could not obtain user benefits—they could only reduce their own costs—and that computers were unlikely to be justified solely for cost reduction.

They produced the table in Figure 3.30, showing their recommendations.

This table shows that only three sorts of benefits were allowed. Unmeasured cost reductions were not candidates for computer applications. Service departments were not allowed to put forward proposals for profit improvements; these had to come from the line departments that would have to achieve them. The distinction between "measured" and "unmeasured" was that a measured benefit occurred when *the person responsible for achieving the benefit accepted the new measured target as his personal*

| | Type of benefit | | |
|---|---|---|---|
| Department | Measured cost reductions | Measured profit improvements | Unmeasured profit improvements |
| Line departments | ✓ | ✓ | Research project |
| Service departments | ✓ | — | — |

**Figure 3.30**

*objective*. The task force recognized that, sometimes, senior management was prepared to say that the possibility of achieving profit improvement looked promising, but no one was prepared to say how much improvement he could get. In such cases, the task force recommended that "research projects" be mounted. These research projects would not involve the purchase of new equipment. The research project would carry out work to establish what the measured benefits would be (using a service bureau, sampling techniques, etc.). The outcome of such research would either be to drop the idea or to take the proposal to a point where a user would accept a measured improvement as his objective—at which time a project involving new equipment could be justified.

## ► Case B

SECURITY

A major bank set up a task force to study the important question of the security of their large computer systems. As part of their studies they conducted a literature search and, as a result, were able to benefit from the published findings[1] of Dr. John Carol, a consultant with the Canadian Privacy and Computers task force. Four hazards were identified, the last two being specific to teleprocessing systems. These hazards and the protection recommended are listed in Figure 3.31.

**Figure 3.31**

| Hazards | Recommended protective action |
|---|---|
| Physical attack | 1. The computing center should be in a secure location, an upper (not top) story without exterior walls. The floors above and below should be under corporate control. |
| | 2. Entry to the computer room should be restricted to operating personnel, and to maintenance technicians and specially designated systems programmers who should work under escort. Entry control should be vested in the operation supervisor on duty, who should keep an entry log. This, and all other logs, should be subject to review by the center's security officer. |

| Hazards | Recommended protective action |
|---------|-------------------------------|
| | 3. The computer records should be in a separate room. Librarians should be on duty for all shifts, and should maintain an input/output log for all removable magnetic media. |
| | 4. Three generations of tape files should be kept, one in the tape library shelves, one in an offsite fireproof vault, the last in a similar facility off site. |
| | 5. A cooperative arrangement with a sister computer in another division or noncompetitive outside firm should be made. |
| Fraud | *Operators* |
| | 1. Never permit one-man operation of computing center. |
| | 2. Segment duties into:<br>Operation supervisor<br>Operators<br>Tape librarians<br>Input, output controller<br>Document control specialists |
| | 3. Counter rotating shifts with some randomness purposely introduced to prevent formation of conspiracies. |
| | 4. Supplement the computer-produced log of work done with one kept by the operator, and have the computer security team audit both. |
| | *Programmers* |
| | 1. Programmers should not operate, and operators should not program. |
| | 2. Programs should be written in modular construction, each module being written by different programmers. |
| | 3. Programmers should write in a language that their boss understands: clear documentation of a program should be a *sine qua non* of any professional programming job. |
| | 4. Program development should be carried out elsewhere than in the principal computing center. |
| | 5. Thorough testing with simulated business data should be required in every case. |
| | 6. Changes in approved programs should only be made after obtaining the approval and signature of the manager of the department. |
| System penetration | 1. Use callback identification in dial-up systems. |
| | 2. Use one-time passwords in hard-wired systems. |
| | 3. Keep log of all transactions at all terminals, and investigate all apparent departures from accepted procedures. |
| Wire tapping | 1. Encipher all transmissions to and from remote terminals. |
| | 2. Program the central computer to function as a high-speed cipher machine and use minicomputers at the remote terminals in a like capacity. |

**Figure 3.31** *(contd)*

► **Case C**

TRANSFER CHARGING

This computer department held the view that computer applications must be beneficial if the users are prepared to pay for them. The department's objectives were to be "profitable," profit being the amount they charged for computer services less their costs. However, they faced certain criticisms from the users concerning the cost of computing. As part of an MBO exercise, a task force was set up to study the transfer-charging system and make recommendations. The following is an extract from a paper they produced:

A spectrum of possibilities exists regarding charging users for computer services, ranging from full cost transfer down to various possible partial systems where certain costs are charged to users and others become part of the general overhead of the company, and, finally, to making no charge to users whatsoever. For the partial systems in the middle of the spectrum, costs may be analyzed as shown in Figure 3.32.

|                   | *Development costs*                                                                                          | *Operating costs*                                        |
| ----------------- | ----------------------------------------------------------------------------------------------------------- | -------------------------------------------------------- |
| Variable costs    | Feasibility studies<br>Systems development<br>Development programming<br>etc.                                | Operators<br>Data preparation<br>Data control<br>etc.   |
| Fixed costs       | Recruitment and training of programmers<br>Accommodation for systems analysts and programmers<br>Program testing, software<br>etc. | Hardware<br><br>Hardware accommodation<br><br>Data preparation equipment<br>etc. |

**Figure 3.32**

This matrix shows that it would be possible to allocate to the users four different "slices" of the computer department's costs, i.e.,

Development costs
Operating costs
Variable or marginal costs
Fixed costs

The pros and cons of various systems within the spectrum of possibilities are described in Figure 3.33.

| Costs to be charged to users | Advantages | Disadvantages |
| --- | --- | --- |
| Full costs | The benefits of computer processing can be measured in the profit and loss analysis of the user departments. | There is no correct or truly equitable method of apportioning all computer costs among users. |
| Development costs | Development costs are truly allocable, being carried out for a particular user. | 1. Users have little control over operating efficiency.<br>2. It is becoming harder to distinguish between development work and work needed to keep systems going.<br>3. It is difficult to charge development costs since they are not known at the start. |
| Operating costs | If development cost is free it encourages full utilization of the computer. | 1. Users have less control over development, and systems may become oversophisticated.<br>2. Operating costs depend on quality of development work. |
| Variable or marginal costs | Also encourages full use of the computer.<br>More equitable to users than charging operating costs. | Marginal cost charging encourages marginal computer applications, which may later lead to unjustified escalation of equipment. |
| None | 1. Simple.<br>2. Most fair, since there is no "correct" system. | 1. Leads to criticism of the computer department as "another overhead."<br>2. Users not interested in the effective use of the computer. |
| Standard costs | Encourages planned level of efficiency. | Standards vary between projects—separate methods engineering required for each project. |
| Profit centers | Can judge computer department alongside the other profit centers in the corporation. | 1. What does "profit" mean for departments which sell to other departments?<br>2. Encourages competition from outside service bureau. |

**Figure 3.33**

Through discussions with various senior people in the computer department, user departments, and accounting department, we have identified the following, often conflicting, objectives for our computer charging system:

To justify the purchase of computer equipment.
To justify the computer applications.
To recover EDP costs from users.
To encourage full use of the computer.
To encourage beneficial use of the computer.
To ensure that users make a profit after meeting their full costs.
To justify the existence of the computer department, i.e., to make a profit or to break even on the services it provides.
To ensure that the computer department is running efficiently.

Since there is no one "correct" charging system—and since each system helps to achieve some of these objectives at the expense of others—we believe the first step is to establish what our objectives for a computer charging system should be. . . .

## ► Case D

### PROJECT PLANNING AND CONTROL

This computer department used systems and programming performance standards which employed certain estimating formulas taken from the generally available literature on this subject. By using this system they had greatly improved their project planning and control; in the days when no one in the department tried to measure how much work would be involved, projects were as long as a piece of string and control almost nonexistent.

They still could not measure systems and programming work with consistent accuracy, however. Sometimes they were right; sometimes projects took twice as long as estimated, or even longer. They established "project management" as one of their key areas. Following their initial studies in this area, they believed that their estimating formulas could be improved and set up a task force with terms of reference to study this problem.

The task force analyzed a large number of sets of estimating formulas advocated by various organizations, and applied them to a number of programs to establish their accuracy. While they established fairly high correlations between certain factors and actual programming time, no system demonstrated a significant correlation between estimated time and the elapsed time of the project—which is the important thing from a management point of view. After further investigation, the team found that this lack of correlation was due to:

1. The varying degree of management effectiveness between programming managers.
2. The novelty present in certain programming tasks, which prevents an estimate of the programming time being made.

Regarding the second point, they found that computer projects frequently break new ground because they involve:

> New hardware
> New software
> New systems (real time, networks, etc.)
> New methods (modular programming, new languages, etc.)
> New requirements (the application may be a new one, or an old one
> which has not been accurately specified before)

Accordingly, they recommended that a new approach to project planning and control be adopted on the following lines:

1. All programming work is recognized as belonging to one of the two following categories:
   Pioneering work
   Measurable work
2. At the outset of any project, all the programming work should be classified into these two categories.
3. Next, the effect of the pioneering work on the project as a whole should be identified, especially:

   When the time taken on pioneering work affects the order of performance of the other tasks; e.g., pioneering variable-length-record software for random access should be done before we write the update programs.

   When the success of pioneering work affects the nature of the work done in other tasks; e.g., failure of variable-length-record software means that we must reorganize our planned file structure.

   What "fail safe" contingencies should be built into the project regarding the probabilities of success of the pioneering work? For example, should we plan at the beginning an alternative record structure which does not "breathe," to allow for the possibility that we may have to use fixed-length records?

4. The pioneering work should be planned and controlled using existing techniques that have proved successful in the management of research and other unmeasurable work.
5. The measurable work should be measured according to our existing formulas but planned according to the analysis of the possible results of the pioneering work (referred to in 3 above).

This is a particularly interesting case study. As one member of the task force said:

> All of us who have worked on computer projects know that much of what we do is really research. But nobody behaves as though it were. The way we control projects here would make you think that everybody expects the equipment and the software to work according to spec and on time, and that the users really know at the beginning what the system should do.

► **Case E**

TERMINALS

This study showed that a valuable part of a task force exercise can be to identify the important questions to ask. A large Canadian oil corporation identified three of its key areas as customer service, operating efficiency, and business control. It was recognized that the efficiency of the corporation's data processing facilities could greatly affect performance in each of these areas. The computer department investigated the present computer-based order processing cycle, and identified the following weaknesses:

Slow response to customer inquiries
Delays in delivery of orders to center
Records updated incorrectly
Suboptimal calculation of economic loads and routes
Prolonged billing cycle

Further investigation led to the view that a computer terminal system would provide important benefits to the corporation in these areas. Since they had no experience with computer terminals, they set up a task force to study the problems of this type of system. As its first job, this task force identified what it believed would be the major problem areas and the key questions that should be asked in each of them (Figure 3.34).

| Problem area | Key questions |
|---|---|
| Teleprocessing software | 1. Should we rely on manufacturers' software for line and terminal control, task management, and store allocation? <br> 2. Should such software offer separate packages or an integrated approach? <br> 3. Can we adjust our applications to the standards of reentrance required by the software? |
| Network design | 1. What line speeds do we require? <br> 2. Should we opt for leased lines or dial-up facilities? <br> 3. Should we multidrop individual terminals or terminal clusters off one line? |
| Polling strategy | 1. Should we poll terminal clusters on each individual terminal? <br> 2. What strategy does each manufacturer adopt? |
| Breakdown of transactions into conversational steps | 1. What will be preserved between the steps? <br> 2. Will the user have to repeat his own identity code and/or the transaction code? <br> 3. Will the preserved data be kept in core or also written to disk? <br> 4. If preserved data is rolled in and out on disk, what volume of disk accesses must be allowed for when calculating the disk queues? |

**Figure 3.34**

| Problem area | Key questions |
|---|---|
| Restart and recovery | 1. What happens when transactions are partly completed at the moment of breakdown? <br> 2. When we restart, do we scratch the steps so far accomplished and start again? <br> 3. How do users know what was their last complete transaction? <br> 4. What happens if the system is down for a whole day? |
| Data management | 1. What record structures, coding conventions, packing and unpacking procedures, and access methods should we use? <br> 2. What effect on disk usage and response time will these standards have? <br> 3. Who should be responsible for designing and implementing such standards? |
| Security | 1. How will we identify users when they are at the terminal? <br> 2. How will we secure unmanned terminals? |
| Standby | 1. Can our operating system be made compatible with that of another data processing center which has agreed to provide standby facilities? <br> 2. What line facilities will we need to the standby center? <br> 3. What reinstatement system will we need to accomplish transfer? |
| Simulation of system performance | 1. Can we simulate our system to anticipate its performance? <br> 2. Can we use existing software to do such simulation? |
| Overall project control | 1. Will our existing planning and control methods cope with a real-time project, since so much of the work breaks new ground? <br> 2. What management techniques are most appropriate? |
| User training | 1. What are the user's training needs? <br> 2. Who will analyze them? <br> 3. Who will plan and implement the user training plan? <br> 4. What methods will we use—especially, can we use terminal equipment operating in a simulation mode? |

**Figure 3.34** (contd)

# Review

This whole process of improving efficiency in the computer department becomes a continuing one through the function of review. The purpose of review is not to criticize poor performance: it has the constructive one of analyzing, in the light of *measured* performance, where our plans were insufficient, and what we need to do in the future.

Therefore, a most important part of the MBO system in the computer department becomes the review session. In fact, many computer departments make it a rule that no more than a quarter of the time will be spent in reviewing *past* performance. Three-quarters of the session is spent in seeing how to get improvements in the future. Typical questions which should be asked at the review session are:

Is this objective still relevant to the business?

Was the results target realistic?

What should we do to close any gaps in performance?

What further improvements should we now go for?

It is useful to distinguish three types of reviews (Figure 3.35):[2]

**Figure 3.35**

| Type | Purpose | Frequency |
|------|---------|-----------|
| Informal, normal management review | This is the regular management process in which the man and his boss assess progress through normal meetings, control data, conversations, and meetings, and take action to remove any obstacles. | As required; may be daily, weekly, etc. |
| Performance review | This is a formal review in which the questions posed are: We agreed on the key results and the job improvement plan. Did we get the planned results? If not, why? What do we plan to do in our next improvement plan? The review is made by the man and his boss and fully discussed, with the results guide they prepared together in front of them. The boss's superior will, in turn, check the review. At least once a year the performance review will include an analysis of what training is needed in order to do the present job better, and the results guide is critically examined and brought up to date. The performance review is a basic business tool, concerned with checking planned results and setting new objectives. | This varies, but a performance review every three months is common. |
| Potential and training review | Quite separately from performance review, it is necessary to consider each man's potential and his training needs. Against the background of his record of performance his strengths and weaknesses can be analyzed: | Annually |

| Type | Purpose | Frequency |
|------|---------|-----------|
| | Is he placed in the most suitable job? Should he be transferred? Is he ready for promotion? If so, when, and what kind of job? Are there personal factors, such as health, to be taken into consideration in planning his career? It is convenient, at the same time, to summarize the manager's training needs in relation to: Present job, as identified in the performance reviews. Possible next job. Changes in company methods, technology, etc., as identified by senior management. The potential and training review is completed by the manager's boss and checked by the boss's superior. The training needs will later be discussed between the manager and his boss. It may be inappropriate to discuss all aspects of potential. If the company employs a personnel manager, he can play a useful role in helping the manager's boss to prepare this review. This is in contrast with the performance review, in which the presence of the personnel manager is inappropriate. | |

**Figure 3.35** (contd)

As we indicated earlier, the frequency of review is quite different for project management. Firstly, three-monthly intervals for the formal review of progress is inadequate for projects, some of which can start and finish within that time. Secondly, reviews take place according to the completion (or noncompletion!) of important project activities, rather than every so often. Review is event oriented rather than time oriented. Thirdly, project review should consider not only the achievement of systems objectives for each activity but also whether we are on time, whether we are within our cost budget, and most important, whether the user benefit aimed for is still achievable.

Fourthly, the terms of reference for the project should be formally reviewed. It is almost possible to say categorically that no project fulfills its original terms of reference. This is because at the beginning it is never possible to see clearly, in a project of any size, what the systems require-ments really are. We learn as we go along. The discipline of detailed systems, design, and programming forces problems into the open which we could not have foreseen during our initial survey. The danger is that when projects change course, as inevitably they must, no one reviews the terms of reference, sets new time and cost objectives, checks that the new requirements are still feasible on the equipment specified and within the run times estimated, and determines whether the user's needs can still be met (or, indeed, whether these needs are still economically justified or relevant). Despite these inevitable and frequently major changes of course, it is surprising how few projects formally review their original terms of reference.

We should, therefore, add a fourth category of review to our earlier chart, as follows:

| Type | Purpose | Frequency |
| --- | --- | --- |
| Project review | To review the progress of computer projects by assessing:<br>1. If the systems objective is still feasible.<br>2. If we are on time.<br>3. If we are within our cost budget.<br>4. If the user benefit is still obtainable, justified, and relevant. | At the target date for each major project activity |
| | Particularly, are the terms of reference for this project still correct and agreed on by the project team, the users, and the computer department? | Every 3 months. |

**Figure 3.36**

### References

1. *Business Quarterly* Autumn 1971.
2. Reproduced from J. W. Humble, *Improving Business Results* McGraw-Hill for Management Centre/Europe, 1965.

# Part 4
# A plan for managing change

## Introduction

Survey and research findings confirm the practical observation that human problems are a major cause of failure in managing the computer effectively. Time and again, an application is technically feasible, makes good economic sense, and then fails dismally at the operational level because of antagonism, ignorance, and simple "cold warfare." Typically, resistance is expressed in terms of:

*Beating the system,* when line managers, rightly or wrongly, perceive the changes as unhelpful or threatening and simply do not cooperate.

► A computer-based stores and spare parts system was introduced into a large mine by specialists, with very little management participation. The underground managers had a long tradition of easy access to stores, with only crude control measures. Faced with the new system, they built up "unofficial" stocks by increasing the number of "lost or damaged" spare parts reported. They requisitioned for unusual specifications, whereas previously they had "made do." By these and other subtle means they brought the computer-based system into administrative difficulties. In the end, the mine was obliged to revert temporarily to the old system while it rethought its approach.

*Blaming the system,* when the computer becomes a convenient scapegoat for things going wrong.

► A foodstuffs corporation computerized its accounting and invoicing system. In the "teething troubles" stage an important customer was sent an inaccurate invoice for an order, which he then canceled. The sales director said that the cancellation was made because of the customer's frustration in dealing with the new ordering and invoicing systems, and the computer department was seriously criticized for causing commercial loss. In fact, the customer was dissatisfied with the quality of the product and had been complaining about this for some months. Poor quality, not inefficient invoicing, was the real cause of the lost order.

*Ignoring the system,* when managers basically continue to use the old information system and ignore the new system, describing it as a load of unnecessary paperwork.

▶ A corporation supplying accessories to the automobile industry decided to use a computer for production control. After two years of effort, the computer produced detailed reordering information for the stores. When the schedules were first produced they were followed blindly by the buying departments. Inevitably, the inventory position worsened, stockouts increased, costs increased, and customer complaints rose seriously. The computer system was discredited, and stores managers were asked to do what they could to improve the situation. Recognizing that the man who issues stock and the buyers often had better knowledge of the local situation than the computer, they instituted a second reorder schedule for "manual corrections." The situation returned to normal. Eighteen months later, when consultants audited the computer system, they found two stock control systems in use. While the computer reordering schedules were apparently being followed, in practice the "manual corrections" form was the one used in *every* case, and the figures were arrived at by using manual methods without any reference to the computer printout. When this was admitted by some of the foremen, they defended their approach by saying, "We tried the computer system but it messed up everything." No attempt was made, by either computer experts or users, to see if a blend of computer prediction and local knowledge could produce a better schedule than either system on its own.

In addition to "user resistance," we find human problems relating to computer experts. Typically, these arise when the specialist pursues technical objectives without full consideration of the overall business interest, i.e., we find human problems in terms of:

*Forcing the system,* where specialists design a system to suit the computer, not necessarily the company.

▶ In a fabrics company that was seeking to automate its order processing procedures, the systems designers saw that four of the present practices stood in the way of a complete computer system. They were: special delivery promises negotiated by the salesmen, nonstandard designs, individual discount rates for overseas customers, and guaranteed color-matching for orders delivered in stages. It was agreed by top management that these facilities would no longer be provided, and the computer system went ahead. No one asked the advice of the marketing department. The new system was forced through from the computer side, and several important customers were lost.

► In another case, the scope of a management system was deliberately reduced so that the computer could cope with it. In an electrical goods manufacturing firm, a very large accounts processing job was seen to be an economic proposition on the computer only if the company ceased to produce invoices for each order and relied instead on just sending a summary statement to its customers at the end of the month. The accounts receivable increased to such an extent (customers paid later and also raised more queries on their accounts) that the extra cost of financing the corporation far outweighed any benefits from the computer system.

It is quite common to regard these and other symptoms, such as poor teamwork between computer specialists and line managers, as superficial problems. All that is required, it is said, is firm direction from top management and more education and training for everyone. In our experience, the problems are more subtle and longer in time span than this simple solution suggests. It is essential to recognize the true complexity of the problems; to develop a planned strategy for managing change; and finally to train and develop people continuously.

## Complexity

The first thing to appreciate is the way in which significant computer installations send ripples of change throughout the whole organization. A new machine tool in the production department may present change problems virtually limited to that department alone. The same could be true, say, of new adding machines in the accounting department. A computer installation, however, must involve many departments and people in even comparatively simple applications. Moreover, the involvement is inevitably challenging. An attempt to write a program will reveal defects in existing definitions and understandings, and expose illogicalities.

► A major automobile components manufacturer decided to use its computer in reviewing its distribution system. The review covered such items as preferred location and sizes of warehouses, and whether to supply certain customers directly or rely on service from local depots. The searching questions, inevitable in the fact-finding stage, revealed a faulty organization structure. Responsibility for distribution was split in a thoroughly confused way between the sales department and the warehouse manager. The latter felt that the revised structure weakened his status and power in the business, and was bitterly resentful of the computer people.

The examples shown below give some idea of the complexity of change brought about by computer systems.

## Examples of changes arising from computer systems

ORGANIZATION

1.  In a large office processing customer orders the number of clerks was reduced. There were fewer supervisory positions, and one horizontal level in the hierarchy was removed. The department manager's job was enhanced in status and responsibility.
2.  In an insurance office, computerization led to a greater degree of centralization in decision making.
3.  In a manufacturing business major disagreement centered on the organizational position of the computer. Originally part of the accounting department, it was now proposed to be transferred to management services.
4.  In a bank much of the work on maintenance of customers' accounts, previously done by the branch managers, was taken away from them and done in regional computer centers.

RELATIONSHIPS

1.  In a chain store business it was felt that one of the computer's major contributions was that it had broken down traditional departmental barriers. Task forces had compelled people to work with a common purpose.
2.  A government department reports that the installation of its computer was a most divisive event, with a running battle going on between specialists trying to force computer systems in and managers determined not to have them.
3.  Virtually every computer application means an additional heavy workload for the managers concerned. Other things get neglected, and irritation and frustration are common.
4.  Computer installations always challenge traditional assumptions. Managers often feel threatened and insecure when weaknesses are exposed, and resentful of those responsible.

CONTROLS

1. Managers in a steelworks complain that they have been overwhelmed by too much data since the computer was introduced—so much so that they rely on the old information system for most decisions.
2. The marketing division of a confectionery business claims that a major increase in its market share was possible only because of the new and rapid analysis of data by the computer system.
3. It was felt by managers in a construction business that computer-based information was too inflexible to deal with the complex variables on a building site.

PLANNING

1. It is well known that there is the incentive to rethink objectives and plans before being able to say what information is necessary. Planning tends to become more formal and disciplined: and sometimes irritatingly rigid and bureaucratic.
2. In a food processing business the release from the burden of clerical labor made time available for long-term innovative planning, and carried the corporation into convenience foods.
3. Time schedules, programs, and procedures within the planning system often become more precise. Managers used to a pragmatic approach feel that the planning system "rules."
4. An international corporation operating a large number of shoe and leather goods repair shop was previously unable to recast its annual budget to show the effect of changes in strategy, pricing policy, or actual performance. With the introduction of a computer, planning became a day to day activity instead of the annual task of "preparing the budget."

## Human conflicts

It is certainly common to find that many people regard the computer as a threatening innovation. Perhaps this arises from the amount of general and uninformed talk and writing over the years about the computer as a replacement for man, about the dehumanizing effect of the computer, and the rather frightening technical jargon and mystique that has been built up around it.

One special change brought about by the introduction of computer systems is that they often introduce unyielding and frustrating rigidity into the situation. Previously, each human being could deal on a "give and take" basis with the other humans involved. Faced with problems in his own area, each man could charm or bully others into doing something special to help. This valuable lubricant is now lost; the computer can be neither charmed nor bullied and applies the rules, irrespective of circumstances. A new standard of discipline and accuracy has to be accepted by those working with computer systems. Such standards often lead to irritation with the computer, a desire to beat the system, and a delight in discovering its every mistake and shortcoming.

Fear and insecurity are invariably aroused by any installation. At one level, the way to minimize this problem is to involve everybody concerned at the earliest possible moment. It seems to be true that human beings who resent bitterly being "chased and manipulated" by others, notably specialists, show a remarkable capacity to change themselves willingly when they become directly involved. A report with recommendations for changes, prepared brilliantly by the computer team, is likely to be received with defensive and critical behavior by operational managers. The same findings might well have been accepted had it been the product of a project team of line managers and computer specialists, working together and educating each other undramatically over a period of time. However, at another level, it must be admitted that major change in business—whether it arises from the computer or a new marketing strategy—will benefit some and not others. A benefit from top management's view may, at a different management level, be seen as an attack on status and personal security. There is a price to pay in human as well as financial terms, for worthwhile breakthroughs. Here again, while the problem cannot be solved (a redundant manager is never going to be happy about it) it can be eased by careful planning. Just who will be affected? What alternative and interesting work can we offer them? How can we help them to adjust to new positions? And so on.

The one important area which does lend itself to vigorous and constructive treatment is the planned provision of knowledge and skills through training. Nothing is more terrifying than the unknown. Many line managers who have been cynical and uncooperative become constructive in outlook after spending some weeks working alongside the computer specialists and attending basic courses on the computer. Many a young computer man has gained new respect for the general management problems of the "user" by being transferred to a line job for some months. Training will be considered in more detail later in Part 4.

## Conflict between operational managers and computer specialists

A great deal has been written in recent years about the continuing tensions and antagonism arising from the different backgrounds and expectations of operational managers and computer specialists. This difference has been described by Michael Rose[1] (drawing on a distinction originally made by A. W. Gouldner) in terms of *cosmopolitans*, e.g., computer men who look outside the organization for their career and their standards of judgment, and operational managers, *locals*, who usually identify with the single organization in which they have spent most if not all of their working lives. The "Average Manager," a distinctive backbone character in every business, has been described by Alastair Mant[2] thus:

> He tends to be in his forties—past the first flush of ambition but not yet on the run home. He does not attract memorable labels ("crown prince," etc.) because his visibility within and without the company is low. . . . He is responsible and willing and has probably made a rational accommodation to limited prospects in the company. He provides the continuity and stability in the infrastructure of the organization, leaving the most spectacular performance and promotion to others. He is basically conservative but still capable of change. . . . Unless he is in line for immediate promotion, he is likely to use new ideas and techniques only so far as he can immediately apply them.

It is likely that Mr. Average Manager will view computer men with suspicion, since they seem long on theory and short on hard experience. They stir things up and are overzealous about changing and challenging established practices.

The "average computer specialist" is likely to be in his thirties. If he is younger he will probably have been in the computer/management science field since he entered business. In formal education terms he will usually be better qualified than Mr. Average Manager. His biggest satisfaction comes from the challenge of analyzing and solving problems—and he is extremely conscious of the potential of the computer, its excitement, its novelty. He gets strong motivation from his work but, unless positively involved in the corporation's problems, may drift into applying his considerable abilities to purely technical problems. He clothes his work in acronymic obscurity, making little sense to some colleagues, let alone the executive managers. He tends to be narrow-minded, and the question "how best to do it" often becomes "how to do it by computer." The best people are scarce, expensive, and mobile—and they know it. They belong to what has been termed the "invisible university" of the computer fraternity. These points are illustrated by some remarks made by a programmer during an interview for a job:

What made you choose programming as your job?

I didn't choose it as a job. I would write programs for a hobby—I wrote programs at college, I write them now in the evenings.

Why are you thinking of leaving your present job?

My project will be over soon—it's going onto the computer in about a month. And you have a time-sharing computer with a real-time project. I want to get some real-time experience.

Your application form shows you've been working for three years, and have had three jobs in this time. This doesn't seem like a good loyalty record.

I feel I'm loyal. I'm loyal to the computer. All these jobs were with computers.

Of course this analysis of the inherent conflict between two "types" is a caricature, and although there is some truth in it, the analysis is too superficial.

In our consulting experience, we find that well over half the computer staff have been recruited and trained from *within* the organization. Apparently a lot of "locals" become "cosmopolitans"! There is certainly growing recognition that, in its early phases, the head of the computer department (or management services) is a key appointment in behavioral terms, and a highly respected "local" line manager is often appointed, backed up by a specialist staff. Moreover, it is naive to assume that a desire for constructive change, breadth of outlook, and capacity to deal with complex conceptual and quantitative issues lie only with computer men. Highly technological businesses, for example, have a high proportion of such managers. And there are certainly some parochial and, in the business sense, narrow-minded computer men around.

Another influence on the relationship between the groups is the type of computer application. Some types, e.g., payroll, have little impact on most managers' key tasks, and they rarely have cause to be deeply involved, pleased, or upset. A major application in an operational area, e.g., production planning and control, clearly offers much more scope for tension.

Finally, a good deal depends on the past history of relationships between "line and staff" and the general sense of mutual respect presently existing. For example, a management services unit that has for many years worked in a useful partnership with line management on work measurement and productivity studies starts off on a solid foundation of goodwill when it "sponsors" the computer.

Perhaps this question of the clash between managers and computer specialists exposes a more fundamental misunderstanding: the idea that conflict is a bad thing which ideally we should prevent from arising.

Conflict between managers and specialists is absolutely inevitable, since the two groups start off with a different set of problems, experience, tools and techniques, and (perhaps) time scale for results. It follows that "bargaining"—trying to sort out these differences and find a common purpose—is always present, too. The challenge for top management is not to stifle conflict but to make sure that it is constructive and fruitful; not to prevent bargaining but to convert "power bargaining" into "creative bargaining." In the former situation, people make early, public commitments to specific positions and use a range of "salesmanship" and threats to get their point over. A certain flair for bluff and brinkmanship is useful in power bargaining. So one hears:

> The computer is definitely not capable of improving my accounting system. I can get the same result without all that fuss. And if you force me to have the new system, I'll not be held responsible for the inevitable setback to our schedules.

And this is countered by:

> Our studies—confirmed by the worldwide experience of the computer manufacturers—show the accounting system to be at present most in-efficient. The computer would reduce costs by one-third without loss of service. Top management must back us on this one. It's really a test case for their support of the computer.

Although common, power bargaining does not necessarily have to occur. With the leadership and example of top management, creative bargaining can become the style. In this approach, great care is taken to avoid starting off with specific commitment and publicity by each side: the focal point is a real and agreed-on business problem. Great care is taken—through task forces, for example—to involve all those deeply concerned. The right spirit exists when the problem is properly analyzed, a range of possible solutions listed and evaluated, and finally the best solution emerges with no one "the winner." This approach is not theo-retical; we use it constantly in our consulting practice. The initial success of the approach, and the speed of instituting it, will vary with the "culture" of each business and the example set by senior management.

## A strategy for learning

As we saw earlier in this book, the important contribution which the computer will make in the future is at the strategic and operational levels of an organization, rather than in cost-saving improvements in existing systems. As this management type of work increases, we can anticipate an acceleration in the growth and complexity of human problems. Clearly, no corporate plan for the computer can be considered complete unless it includes thoughtful and specific plans for managing change.

*Plan* is a word to be stressed. This work is too important commercially, let alone in human terms, to be left to chance. While every situation is different, certain guidelines have emerged from our experience. They can be expressed as a six-point program:

1. Securing top management's commitment.
2. Understanding the basic behavioral issues.
3. Clarifying objectives.
4. Ensuring that communications are effective.
5. Planning for growth and renewal.
6. Using a "change agent" constructively.

## 1. Securing top management's commitment

Top management's personal example, involvement, and leadership lie at the heart of managing change. Their philosophy, manifest in daily action and decisions, will set the tone for resistance or cooperation. It is easy to preach that others need to communicate frankly and openly; but is top management genuinely receptive to the criticisms which may be implied by a major computer feasibility study? Equally important, does top management recognize that it cannot secure participation, teamwork, commitment, and so on, merely by *telling* people that this is how they must behave?

> ▶ The president of an insurance company called together his top 15 managers and his new computer manager. He said, "After careful consideration, the board has decided to introduce a computer into this business. Mr. X has been brought in from another company as the computer manager and he will be telling you, stage by stage, just what you must do in order to get full value from this new investment. I know I can count on your full interest and cooperation in doing as he asks." It is difficult to think of a more unfortunate way for the new computer manager to meet his colleagues. Of course, they all said the right things on the day . . . but privately they regarded the new man as a threat, not a helper.

Top management's commitment and involvement are important at every stage. During feasibility studies, they must recognize the profound long-term influence which the computer may have on the business, and provide this wide framework of reference to the study team. Visits should be made to comparable installations, and frank exchanges held with senior people about problems and benefits. An orientation course on the management implications of the computer is highly desirable, since without this, or previous experience with computers, it is not easy to ask the right searching questions when the report is submitted. At the design stage, a major concern is to set the climate for creative bargaining and harness inevitable conflict into constructive change. One major "sacrifice" which may well be behaviorally influential is top management's decision to allocate people "too good to be spared" to be trained to run the computer. And, of course, top management must insist on the same high level of profit planning, budgeting, and control as for any other commercial project. At the "running in" stage, top management may well not be involved. What they should do is provide the organizational and human resources needed for the project to succeed and—very hard in practice!—show continued positive enthusiasm and determination in the face of inevitable setbacks and disappointments. Recognition of the heavy extra workload undertaken by some managers at this time is also frequently overlooked.

Finally, we should recognize that, particularly in large organizations, it is extraordinarily difficult for top management to have a feel for the realities of human problems deep in the business. John Gardner's comment[3] is truly perceptive:

> As organizations (and societies) become larger and more complex, the men at the top (whether managers or analysts) depend less and less on firsthand experience, more and more on heavily "processed" data. Before reaching them, the raw data—what actually goes on "out there"—have been sampled, screened, condensed, compiled, coded, expressed in statistical form, spun into generalizations and crystallized into recommendations.
>
> It is a characteristic of the information processing system that it systematically filters out certain kinds of data so that these never reach the men who depend on the system. The information that is omitted (or seriously distorted) is information that is not readily expressed in words or numbers, or cannot be rationally condensed into lists, categories, formulae, or compact generalizations by procedures now available to us. . . .
>
> . . . . It filters out emotion, feeling, sentiment, mood, and almost all of the irrational nuances of human situations. It filters out those intuitive judgments that are just below the level of consciousness.
>
> So the picture of reality that sifts to the top of our great organizations and our society is sometimes a dangerous mismatch with the real world. We suffer the consequences when we run head on into situations that cannot be understood except in terms of those elements that have been filtered out. The planners base their plans on the prediction that the people will react in one way, and they react violently in quite another way.

## 2. Understanding basic behavioral issues

Surely, true and lasting behavioral change, as compared with lip service and superficial attitudes, arises from viewing the introduction of the computer as essentially an occasion to *learn together*. The issues are too complex for one group to solve alone. Commitment comes from sharing in the process of deciding where and how to use the computer, and everyone has some experience or ideas to put into the pool of knowledge.

We need a determined learning strategy to ensure that the structure, relationships, and values of the computer, as well as its technical and economic feasibility, are appropriate. If change concentrates in one department, there is not enough leverage to overcome the inevitable inertia. *All* the managers affected must be involved. This may appear obvious, but in our experience it is a rare viewpoint. Usually, the philosophy is "tell them and sell them," and run a few brief computer orientation seminars for good measure. Consider some of the basic behavioral issues and their relevance to the computer.

*What motivates people?* At a crude level it is argued: "We are going to introduce a computer, and since it particularly affects department A and they are likely to be difficult, we will guarantee them no redundancy and offer them a bonus when the new scheme is operating to standard." We know from experience and behavioral science studies that this is a naively narrow viewpoint.

Abraham Maslow[4] taught us that motivation essentially comes from within an individual: he seeks continuously to reach certain goals because he has basic, internally generated needs. Maslow identified a simple hierarchy of needs:

> Need for self-actualization
> Need for esteem
> Need for belongingness and love
> Safety needs
> Physiological needs

His argument is that these are needs of an ascending order: no one is going to be particularly concerned with creative work if he is cold and hungry.

Certainly, with "knowledge people" in the computer field the highly motivating influence of "self-actualization" is quite evident, and one must plan to provide opportunities for it. Two of the common reasons why the computer department labor turnover is so high are:

> There is no opportunity to use my knowledge and skill to their fullest extent (*self-actualization*).

and

> The computer people just aren't respected in this place. All we get is complaints about overhead burdens and so on. I'm quitting (*need for esteem*).

Frederick Herzberg[5] takes this analysis a step further. In research on the job attitudes of accountants and engineers—and now with many other groups in different countries—he found that a pattern of factors emerged, some satisfying to the individual and some dissatisfying.

The *satisfiers* or *motivators* are:

Achievement
Recognition
Work itself
Responsibility
Advancement
Growth

The *dissatisfiers* or *hygiene* factors are:

Company policy and administration
Supervision
Working conditions
Interpersonal relations (with supervisors, subordinates, and peers)
Salary
Status
Job security
Personal life

In Herzberg's view, the dissatisfiers or hygiene factors are deficit needs, in that their importance is felt only in their absence. For example, people take good working conditions for granted and do not get any particular satisfaction from them. However, bad working conditions are frequently a source of dissatisfaction. In many progressive computer departments, most of the hygiene factors are already present. The real challenge is, therefore, to provide self-fulfillment for achievement-motivated employees. Job enrichment is the theme which emerges—i.e., a planned effort to increase the challenge of a job so that a man can grow in skill, responsibility, and feeling of accomplishment.

With regard to the average computer installation, there are two obvious conclusions to be drawn from Herzberg's work. Firstly, the reason for the sharp rise and fall in morale among computer staff, frequently leading to high staff losses, is that the "satisfiers" are only provided on a temporary basis. During the initial development of a computer system they are present to a high degree. As soon as the main systems become operational and have to be maintained, the satisfiers largely disappear. Moreover, since advancement is often seen in the limited terms of "promotion within the computer department," it is rarely a motivator. A widened vision of opportunity to advance to different kinds of work in the whole organization would transform motivation in this respect. It is also clear that, in the face of high labor turnover or a disgruntled group of specialists, the analysis of the cause of malaise rarely gets beyond hygiene factors.

Secondly, one of the main reasons for users' antagonism toward the computer is that they fear, sometimes with justification, that the computer system will destroy their "satisfiers." They feel that once a computer system is installed, they will lose their opportunity for achievement. Their work will become routine and constrained within the rules and standards instituted by automation. With the removal of discretion, the responsibility will go out of their jobs.

This whole question of motivation leads to a wider behavioral issue about the *style of management* to be followed. By far the most influential behavioral scientist in our lifetime was the late Douglas McGregor. In his famous book *The Human Side of Enterprise*,[6] McGregor insisted that management is a profession; and since a manager's main job is to manage other people in achieving the organization's objectives, knowledge of the behavioral sciences is essential. This simple statement has immediate relevance to computer departments, in which the key people are predominantly oriented toward technical and organizational matters. It is a rare senior computer man who has made a systematic study of human problems. The result is that relationships with managers in user departments are often unnecessarily strained, and internal morale is frequently low. McGregor believed that the starting point in choosing an appropriate management style was to have a set of beliefs about the nature of people. To illustrate this he described two theoretical views:

*Theory X* is the conventional and traditional way of viewing people in an organization. Essentially,

> The average human being has an inherent dislike of work and will avoid it if he can.
>
> Because of man's dislike of work, he must be coerced, controlled, directed, or threatened with punishment to get him to put forth adequate effort toward the achievement of organizational objectives.

> The average human being prefers to be directed, wishes to avoid responsibility, has relatively little ambition, and wants security above all.

*Theory Y* is a theoretical structure built on behavioral research. Essentially,

> The expenditure of physical and mental effort in work is as natural as play or rest.
>
> External control and the threat of punishment are not the only means of getting men to work toward the organization's objectives. Men will exercise self-direction and self-control toward achieving objectives to which they are committed.
>
> Commitment to objectives is a function of the rewards associated with their achievement (esteem and self-actualization, for example).
>
> Under the proper conditions, average human beings learn not only to accept but to seek responsibility.
>
> Most people are capable of a relatively high degree of imagination, ingenuity, and creativity in solving organizational problems.
>
> Under the conditions of contemporary life, the average person's intellectual potentialities are being utilized only partially.

McGregor did not say that either theory was right or wrong, and indeed recognized a whole range of intermediate possibilities. As his colleague Edgar Schein wrote, "He wanted theory Y to be a realistic view, in which one examined one's assumptions, tested them against reality and then chose a managerial structure that made sense in terms of one's diagnosis of reality. . . ."

From our viewpoint, McGregor provides a practical starting point for those directly concerned with the computer—managers and specialists—to think through their views on management style. Just what approach will meet the unique situation in their organization at *that* time and with *those* people? Far from being academic, such a discussion is of the greatest practical importance. If one believes that creativity is widespread, it makes good sense to tap the ideas of many people; if one believes that people will dodge responsibility if they possibly can, then clearly it is necessary to direct them very closely. Should one proceed on the basis that self-control must be used to the maximum possible extent, or that close control by the boss is correct? Without some agreement on these issues, it is most difficult to build a strategic plan for managing change.

## TEAMWORK

Every computer project is deeply concerned with teamwork. Consider some examples:

A task force of the general manager, chief accountant, marketing manager, and computer manager is set up to analyze the present use of the computer, and to search key business areas for profitable opportunities for more effective use.

Within the computer department, it is found necessary to move the computer's location from site X to site Y. A working party of five people is established to plan the best layout of the new site, and to program the physical movement with minimum disruption.

A team, consisting of the purchasing director, computer manager, and finance director, is working to examine the scope for computerizing purchasing in a department store.

In order to implement an order processing computer system, an engineering components manufacturer formed a project team consisting of members representing all the departments involved—the computer department, sales, order processing, stock control, purchasing, and manufacturing.

For each of its projects, a large bank formed a new project team drawn from a pool of system analysts and programmers. The team disbanded after each project and returned to the pool.

Task forces, teams, project teams, working parties—there is a wide range of titles and functions, but what is common is a group of people meeting together, often for the first time as a team, to solve a problem. Some of the things that go wrong in these teams include:

Failure to identify clearly, to mutually agree on, and to understand the primary results which the team is expected to produce.

A team that does not represent the best mix of disciplines, experience, and viewpoints. A team might, for example, be dominated by technical people, with the result that the users' needs are not fully clarified.

Poor organization of the team effort, such as an overly quick identification of an issue, and then discussion concentrated on this. In practice, it may be better to take more time to identify a range of issues, then to rank them in terms of priority. Conversely, some teams are so sensitive to the need to plan how they will work together that they spend more time talking about this than solving the real problem. Another example of bad team organization is the failure to monitor progress toward the desired result, so there's a "crisis" as the deadline for recommendations looms closer.

Inadequate interpersonal and social skills within the team. Often, much that is said in the group is misinterpreted because it is phrased in technical jargon ("I think a modular, multiresponse Mark 700 widget software package is the answer to this problem"). Some people contribute in cryptic monosyllables; some bore the group with long-winded, overelaborate statements. Perhaps it is more important to recognize the problems arising from what is *not* said.

Faced with mistrust or insecurity, members are simply not going to place on the table their real and full viewpoint. Or they direct what they say to someone who they believe will be in sympathy with their opinions: an analysis of one computer project team showed a very high flow of exchange between executive manager and executive manager, computer specialist and computer specialist; but virtually no cross-exchange.

It is also worth stressing that teams should be used selectively and only when the result achieved is likely to be better than it would be if the task were allocated to an individual manager. After all, teams cost time and money. The current fashion of setting up teams on the slightest pretext is not only wasteful but overlooks the power of *individual* accountability and motivation. As Douglas McGregor said:

> Perhaps it is now clear why an effective management team seldom just happens. It is a complex and delicate system, the building and maintenance of which requires much time and attention. Its contribution to the achievement of the goals of the enterprise can, however, be well worth the effort devoted to its creation.

Later in Part 4, we will describe a practical approach to team training.

Having secured the support of top management, and understood the basic behavioral issues, we will briefly summarize four other aspects of the program.

## 3. Clarifying objectives

Throughout this book, we have constantly stressed the need to set out clear objectives: what is to be achieved, by what standard or criterion, by what date and at what cost? If this is valid for financial, production, and marketing computer applications, it is just as true of setting objectives for the human resources required. We are thinking about:

> How many computer specialists, with what skills and experience, will we need to fulfill our plans for the computer?

> How many can be promoted from within, and how many do we need to recruit externally?

> Do we know enough about the achievement, experience, expectations, knowledge, and skills of our own people to plan for succession and for their career development?

> What new knowledge and skills will nonspecialist managers need to have about the computer if they are going to be equipped to contribute and cooperate in the planned applications?

> What are our internal training capabilities? What do we know about the range and quality of outside courses?

These and many questions like them need to be answered in a disciplined way before clear "human resources" objectives can be established.

## 4. Ensuring that communications are effective

Again, this requires an analytical approach and a clear plan. Just how will we make sure that everyone knows what he or she should do about the computer installation, how it will affect them, how it is progressing, and so on? How can we ensure that the communication flow is not just top-to-bottom but involves higher levels "listening" to what lower levels have to contribute? And what about horizontal communications, particularly the flow between specialists such as computer people and line managers?

Each company will develop its own methods. These range from briefing meetings, to written bulletins, to "computer progress" as an item on the agenda of regular management meetings, to visits by people to the computer department and vice versa. There is no shortage of methods and techniques—the real problems arise from a misunderstanding of the whole communication process. It is usually assumed that people are entirely logical and that if a rational case is communicated to them sensibly, they will accept it. A computer application will reduce costs and improve information flow and accuracy: therefore, line managers involved are bound to be appreciative once they fully understand. However, these managers may be so conditioned by their past experience that they perceive "the message" in terms of an established framework of expectations and values. They largely see what they expect to see and hear what they expect to hear.

This point is illustrated delightfully by Dr. John Burton, Director of the Centre for the Analysis of Conflict, University College, London:

> A male driver approaches a bend on a narrow road. He is suddenly con-
> fronted by an approaching car which swerves out of his way at the last
> moment. The driver, a woman, appears agitated and as she passes the man,
> leans out of her window and shouts "pig." The man, perceiving that insult
> has been added to near injury, angrily responds with "cow." As he turns
> the bend, he is obliged to maneuver skillfully to avoid a pig wandering in
> the road. The man, later reflecting on the incident, is amused at the co-
> incidence that he had nearly run into a real pig so soon after that cow of a
> driver had called him a pig.

This apocryphal story shows that the frame of reference of the male driver, i.e., his predisposition to perceive all women drivers as incompetent, caused him to attribute her swerve to bad driving, to misperceive her warning, and to fail, even in the light of subsequent experience, to correct his misperception.

Although communication is generally regarded as "projecting a message," it is well to realize that communication has not taken place until someone has received the message, perceived how it relates to his own experience, and thus understood it.

> ▶ In one firm, a major "sales campaign" for the computer and all it might do for the company was imaginatively launched. The project was given a name—a well-publicized acronym—and illustrated with brochures, films, and so on. Managers thought that the benefits were exaggerated and the difficulties deliberately understated. A serious credibility gap developed and persisted for a long time.

## 5. Planning for growth and renewal

Since the computer is at the heart of change in a business, the original assumptions, objectives, and communication systems which were excellent, say, for early applications, may become bureaucratic or inappropriate at later stages. Quite simply, planning involves recycling and rethinking what is needed tomorrow and not just repeating yesterday's successes. Although this is a general truth, it has special relevance to the computer. Early work is not just technical—even more, it is educational. Working together on a real project, the computer specialists and line managers learn from one another. New and rewarding applications, which neither group alone could have perceived or become emotionally ready to work on, now become possible. Mutual respect, self-confidence, a sense of achievement, all combine to raise expectations and standards. In this sense, the intelligent use of the computer is a continuing process of growing knowledge, commitment, and renewal of purpose. It is an organic adaptation to a changing environment rather than the usual pattern of long periods of *status quo* punctuated by violent or revolutionary change.

## 6. Using a "change agent" constructively

A recurring theme of the behavioral scientists is the valuable contribution which can be made by an outside "change agent." Sometimes the man fulfilling this role is described as a catalyst or as an MBO adviser or consultant. It is, perhaps, the most constructive client/consultant relationship of all. Basically, the change agent fulfills the following roles:

> As a member of task forces, project teams, board meetings, and so on, he should provoke thought and self-criticism by asking searching questions.

Through the breadth of his outside experience he can provide comparison with "the best practice elsewhere," which can cause the team to raise its level of expectations. It is not his job to diagnose a problem *alone* and then "tell the client what to do." Rather, he is sharing with his client a different viewpoint, knowledge, and experience. Together, they can produce a diagnosis and range of solutions which are better than either could do alone.

He is a teacher in the sense that he may have unique knowledge or skills not available within the organization. It is his job to communicate this knowledge to his client, formally or informally, as fast as he can, so that the client's dependence on him is reduced as quickly as possible. For example, a change agent may have great experience in the various methods of MBO—defining objectives, key results analysis, review of performance and potential. He passes on this knowledge by holding briefing sessions for all the managers, and by training several members of the client staff in depth and supervising them in their early applications.

Or the change agent may have a special knowledge in advanced methods of programming. He will work with the client staff, teaching them his skills and guiding them until they are independent. But his main contribution is *not* in the special knowledge he brings to the problem. Frequently, members of the team will be more knowledgeable in their own field than he. His chief asset is that he is not involved in the conflict, which we have seen is an inevitable and vitally important part of any change. As an outsider, with enough knowledge and experience to appreciate all sides of the problem, he can ensure that good ideas get aired and acted upon, whether they come from the top or the bottom of the management hierarchy. By listening to the arguments, which may be largely based on self-interest he can extract the logic of the situation. While he may be conditioned by his own past experience and environment, it is not the same experience and environment as that shared by those within the corporation, and his perception of the situation should bring fresh slants on the problem.

He is an evaluator in the continuing sense of providing an objective opinion of progress and problems after his initial major input. This long-term, part-time relationship is of special value to the client. Usually, in the effective computer context the change agent is fulfilling two roles simultaneously. He is the catalyst for diagnosing and solving such human problems as resistance to change, integrating individual and organizational goals, suggesting ways to manage and resolve conflict, and adapting the structure to meet new goals. He is also contributing knowledge on the managerial and technical problems inherent in making the computer effective.

In our experience, these roles are complementary: to be a change agent in behavioral terms alone may be to create a purposeful organization doing the wrong things with enthusiasm. To be a change agent in technical and managerial terms alone may be to identify objectives and opportunities for the computer to make a major contribution, and yet to lose this potential through insensitivity and an amateurish approach to basic human and behavioral problems.

# Training and development

Most organizations have not yet begun to grapple with the problem of systematic training in knowledge, skills, and behavior to ensure that their computer is effectively used. Consider, for example,

1.  The sheer scale of the training problem in ensuring that, in every organization in which computers are or soon will be installed, the existing managers appreciate what the computer is and what it can or cannot do for them.
2.  "Unbundling" by computer manufacturers has forced companies to recognize that the purchase of a machine no longer automatically gives free or very cheap training.
3.  The problem of training newly appointed line managers in computer systems:

    ▶ In a market research firm, which was among the pioneers of business computers many years ago, it was recently found that those line managers who had been appointed after the computer system had been designed and implemented did not know the rules which the computer followed in operating the systems for which they were responsible.

4.  The challenge of teaching computer specialists enough about general management to enable them to contribute maturely and effectively to solving strategic problems of the business.
5.  The complexity of upgrading computer people to fit them for rapid growth in responsibility and promotion inside and outside the computer department.

Most organizations, however, are investing far too little money and effort in training.

## 1. The training process

One useful approach to this difficult training problem is to use a simple model, as in Figure 4.1.

This model is developed in more detail in Figure 4.2. Let us consider it in relation to the computer.

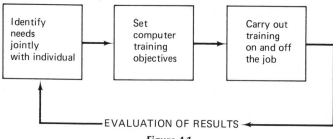

**Figure 4.1**

TRAINING NEEDS ANALYSIS

PRESENT JOB. Each manager—specialist or executive—has a specific set of objectives to achieve, and this is typically summarized in his key results analysis and job improvement plan. Some examples of these were given in an earlier section on the efficient computer department. At regular intervals, the job holder and his boss will sit down together and carry out a review of performance. From this discussion may be demonstrated a gap between results expected and results actually achieved. Although not the only possible explanation, the failure to reach agreed performance standards *may* stem from lack of knowledge or skills.

An example of needs arising from the present job is given in Figure 4.3. In the review session with this man, his performance was measured objectively against previously agreed standards. It was found that this man's team was doing excellent work. There were fewer user complaints concerning his team's projects than any others, and less time spent on subsequent maintenance. The time he needed for parallel running was also considerably better than the agreed objectives. Nevertheless, he consistently failed to meet the original target dates. During discussion it was agreed that he had difficulty in estimating in advance the amount of work involved. He also experienced delays due to emergency calls on his programmers, and overloaded his best programmers with impossible targets, frequently leaving the weak programmers idle. His training needs were identified as shown in Figure 4.3. He attended two short outside courses. Following these courses he and his boss discussed ways of improving the situation in their own firm. They designed a system of modular programming which would give him greatly improved flexibility in work scheduling—since he would be giving out smaller parcels of work—and enable him to utilize the weaker programmers more effectively by isolating the simple work. He then worked with outside consultants on the detailed design of such a system and its initial implementation.

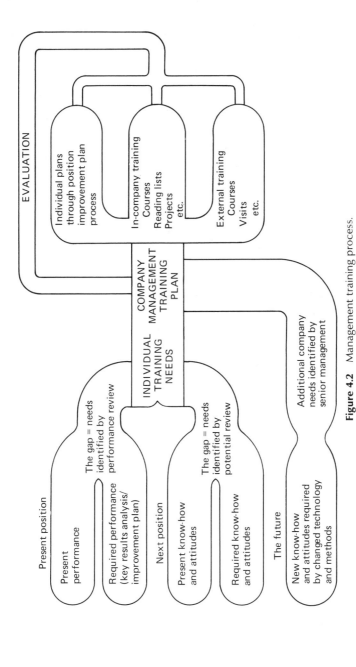

**Figure 4.2** Management training process.

---

*Present job—training needs*

Name: A. Brightman
Job:     Senior programmer
Date:

| Performance gap summary | Training needs | Training | Job improvement plan |
|---|---|---|---|
| 1. Continually failing to meet target dates | 1.1. Work scheduling and control | Resources planning course (four days) | Introduce modular programming |
| | 1.2. Management of programmers | Man management course (one week) | |
| etc. | | Discussion with boss once a month | |

---

**Figure 4.3**

During the next year, his experience in operating the system, modifying it, and reviewing its progress gave him the sort of on-the-job training which enabled him to overcome this problem completely.

NEXT JOB. A part of the review procedure is to consider the kind of job the man might do next: this may be a range of work rather than one specific job. While the corporation's view of the man's future is very important, it should be recognized that "knowledge workers," in particular, are motivated by an opportunity to say what *they* want to do. Indeed, the failure to listen to what people want to do with their lives can lead a firm to present a training and career plan which is at once rejected by the man. There should be a dialogue, not a monologue with the boss telling the man what he must do next. The outcome of these discussions, which might usefully involve people other than man and boss, can be summarized as shown in Figure 4.4.

For his present job, the concern was to put right his weaknesses; for his next job, the emphasis was to build on his strengths. This analysis of strengths should concentrate as much as possible on objective judgment based on measurements of performance. Compare

> I am impressed with this man's ability. He has an extremely high intelligence, and displays great ingenuity in problem solving. He works hard and seems to thrive on being given the really large and difficult programs to write.

with

> This man has not missed a target date in the last four years.

Name: A. Brightman
Date:

Next job—training needs

| Strengths | Personal likes, ambitions | Next job | Training needs | External training | Internal training plan |
|---|---|---|---|---|---|
| Flair for systems specification: average three days only lost on systems queries in the last four projects. Gets on well with users: no user complaints, both X and Y specifically asked for him on the last project. Got ten A's and four B+s from the audience on the last management appreciation course we gave. Excellent computer system designer: only one program suite needed subsequent redesign, and the Mark II running times for this suite improved on the original times by only 8 per cent. | Liaising with users. Especially discussing their requirements. Wants systems analysis. | Systems analyst | 1. Systems analysis. | — | Perform critical appraisal of the current systems analysis manual. |
| | | | 2. Manual systems design. | O and M, including clerical work measurement (three weeks) | Take over premium-bonus section supervisor's job for six months. |
| | | | 3. Benefits of EDP. | — | |
| | | | 4. Managing human control systems. | | |

**Figure 4.4**

Both these statements are taken from actual review forms.

Returning to Figure 4.4, note the column for ambition. "What do *you* want to do?" is not always asked at informal review sessions. This needs analysis is based on the key results analysis of this man's next job if it is clearly defined at this stage. What does he need, in addition to his present knowledge and skills, to do these key tasks? No satisfactory external training could be found for basic systems analysis (as distinct from computer systems analysis), for identifying the benefits of EDP, or for managing human control systems. Internal training plans were the important ones, however, and included job rotation, i.e., doing a clerical management job for six months, and studying and appraising the present systems analysis methods.

COMPANY NEEDS. So far, we have thought of needs in relation to individuals. There is a total company view on training needs also. Take this simple case. A corporation intends to install a computer next year but has not yet communicated this information to all levels of management. It is, therefore, impossible for managers in their normal reviews of performance and potential to identify the needs arising from the computer installation. It is a central responsibility to plan such changes of training initially.

In another case, a firm which already has a computer appraised the key area "electronic data processing" with respect to the forward corporate objectives and the present and forecastable trends in technology, attitudes, resource availability, etc. The study of the key trends showed beyond doubt that more and more of the corporation's control procedures would be carried out by computers. Nevertheless, it was apparent that the new managers in the corporation (those occupying new posts since the introduction of EDP) did not know what the EDP system did, and seemed unable to get to know. There was a growing disappointment with the results achieved by the computer.

The long-term training needs for the corporation were identified as an improvement, for all management and computer staff, of their understanding of what computers could and should do for the corporation, and how they should be managed and fitted into the organization structure.

They needed to develop their methods and attitudes when it came to working together in teams, and it was recognized that little could be done externally to provide this training. Accordingly, the company set up a series of mixed computer/user task forces to study key areas of the business and to see how formal control might help to attain the company's objectives. The aim was that all present and potential managers, systems analysts, and senior programmers would work on one such task force within the next four years. Each task force began its operations by having a consultant counsel them on team effectiveness. This needs analysis is illustrated in Figure 4.5.

Key Area: Electronic data processing
Date:

| Relevant corporate objectives | Key trends and symptoms | Training needs | Methods |
|---|---|---|---|
| 1. To continue to achieve a return on capital of 13 per cent after tax on total assets. <br> 2. To achieve a growth rate of 11 per cent per annum. <br> 3. To hold the present level of administrative and overhead costs for the next two years. <br> 4. To diversify into earthworking equipment. <br> 5. To extend markets into the under-developed countries. <br> etc. | 1. Increase in the volume of formal control relative to informal control. <br> 2. New management unaware of what the formal control systems do and unable to get this knowledge. <br> 3. Disappointment with EDP. | 1. Improved perception by computer experts and management of the role of the computer in the company. <br> 2. Improved teamwork. | 1. Set up computer task forces. <br> 2. Obtain behavioral science training. |

**Figure 4.5**   Company training needs.

## 2.  Three examples of good training

Three examples of good training are discussed below, in the areas of: team training; in-house, project-based training; and perceptive use of outside courses.

▶ TEAM TRAINING[7]

A corporation set up a task force of computer manager, senior systems analyst, works manager, and production planner to examine the computer's contribution to production planning and control. These people had never before worked together as a team. At their first meeting, the team was

given a brief lecture by a consultant, on essential concepts such as perception, communication, status and goals, and the program for their application.
This initial coaching and development effort utilized several exercises which
helped break the ice, and which introduced the principles of effective
teamwork.

Development continued as the group went about its normal business,
the consultant observing and classifying the behavior of the members. He
fed back his observations in a standard format at intervals and guided the
group members toward patterns of behavior appropriate to the achievement of the group goal. The activities and working methods of the members,
and the group problems they faced, were continually related to their
personal objectives and the purposes of the group.

The problems associated with the practice of systematic teamwork were
handled and resolved as group members learned to pattern their work in
line with the steps of the following model.

**Figure 4.6**

The group's attention was drawn to inadequate goal discussions: Did they
all have the same understanding of their goals? Did they share them?

They were asked to concentrate on their preparation for discussion: Had
they identified as many of their tasks as they could before they started
discussion?

They were also encouraged to monitor their working: Was the goal
realistic? Were all the tasks identified? Was the planning sensible? Were
tasks allocated to the right people?

Since the coaching effort proceeded concurrently with the group's
legitimate activities, the resultant increase in pace, and improvement in
the marshaling of talent, paid immediate dividends in time saved, improvement in decisions taken, plans prepared, and so on. Group members
formed impressions of how their contributions were received, who was
"difficult," who spoke for the greatest length of time, and so on; but these

impressions were generally too vague to form a basis for positive action. Indeed, even when impressions were quantified, the action the group should take to "work more effectively together" was not clear.

An important requirement of this team training system is, therefore, the classification of the social behavior exhibited in a group. There is also a requirement for a set of principles to allow for evaluation of the picture of the group's activities which emerges, against the background of the goals the group is attempting to achieve.

A system called interaction analysis, which satisfies both requirements, was used. This system enables all group behavior to be classified; it has 12 categories such as "shows antagonism," "asks for opinion," "gives suggestions," "gives orientation."

The first stage in the application of interaction analysis involved observation of the group at work over a series of sample periods. The contributions were classified, and a note was taken of who initiated and who received each contribution. The data was processed by means of a computer terminal, and a detailed picture of the social life of the group was quickly available for feedback to the group members.

The problems associated with social processes were resolved as group members, with the help of the consultant, explored the appropriateness of such things as:

A very low rate of questioning when highly technical matters were being discussed.

The dominance of a few individuals when the group was seeking a lasting consensus.

Very little disagreement when conflict of interest was apparent.

A high incidence of opinion swapping rather than full exploration of individual judgments as they came up.

Certainly, it was our experience that the computer task force concerned was much more effective than similar groups which did not have the benefit of team training. The really important benefit perceived by members was that they were helped positively to solve real problems and were not playing games.

▶ IN-HOUSE PROJECT-BASED TRAINING[8]

A corporation manufacturing photographic goods and materials had used computers for data processing for seven years. During this time it had automated most of its routine control systems and changed its equipment from second to third generation. The costs involved had been high and the benefits uncertain. There was the usual evidence of frustration on the part of users of the system who had lost control of part of their work and whose real requirements were not being met. They were told that the changes in the system that they wanted were "too expensive," "technically impossible," and "beyond the capacity of the team of analysts and programmers who were completely loaded with present commitments." Typically, the computer staff were equally frustrated, their projects were being delayed for "lack of user cooperation," and their ideas for systems improvements were frequently rejected because the suggestions involved fresh equipment and "nobody here seems to understand that these things cost money."

Clearly, progress would only be made with this problem by improving the managers' appreciation of what computers could and could not do for the business, and by improving the ability of the computer staff to analyze and contribute to the needs of the corporation. But the firm had already invested very considerable amounts of time and money in sending its managers and computer staff to outside computer courses: management appreciation courses, systems analysis courses, and the like. The main limitations of such courses were identified as:

> Low relevance of course content to the detailed problems the staff faced in making effective use of computers in their corporation.

> Difficulty in getting the *whole group* of people involved with the day-to-day computer projects and systems to change their behavior and attitude.

The firm decided to adopt an in-house approach to training. The first in-house computer training project took the following form:

**i.  Appointment of course leader.** An outsider was appointed as course leader.

**ii.  Analysis of training needs.** The course leader helped make an analysis of the corporation's computer training needs. This took four weeks. During this time, computer training needs were identified under three headings: attitude, knowledge, and skills. This needs analysis revealed, among other things:

ATTITUDES

Top management: that computers should save staff costs.

User management: that the computer had been imposed on them; that it was really a machine for doing fast mathematical computations and was not relevant to their work; that it would increase the control imposed on them by the accountant and head office; that automation was something they had to learn to live with.

Supervisors, clerks, work force: that the computer was an uncompromising control system to be fed with data and ignored as much as possible.

Data processing manager: that it was only a question of time and the retirement of certain of the present management force before the computer virtually controlled the firm.

Data processing staff: that their job was to redesign existing control systems so that it was technically feasible to process them on a computer; that if projects were technically feasible they should be implemented; that if this corporation did not continue its policy of pioneering new computer equipment they would probably leave.

Generally: an attitude of "we/they" between the computer department and the rest of the firm.

## KNOWLEDGE GAPS

Generally: the fundamentals concerning the difference between mechanized and human control.

On the part of the users: the scope and limitations concerning mechanized control provided by present-day data processing equipment; the detail of the corporation's existing computer systems.

On the part of computer experts: an appreciation of the key areas of the business and the key decisions to be taken; the effect of man/machine control systems on the humans involved with the system; the contents and meaning of the corporation's balance sheet and profit and loss account.

## SKILLS LACKING

Analysis methods concerning key areas, decisions, and the scope for automation; design methods concerning the description of control systems; methods for improving the effectiveness of study groups; project control methods; control of experts; methods concerning program maintenance and improvement.

**iii. Design of the course.** Following the above analysis the course leader advised concentration on the following topics:

Improving the effectiveness of group study and group behavior.
Management by objectives.
Control theory: human control in practice; mechanized control in practice.
Principles of leadership and organization.
Decision analysis.
The structure of information.
Quality control in computer programs.
The company's financial and cost accounting figures.
Computer and data-capture equipment and capability.

In association with those concerned, he then designed for the corporation an "effective computer" course. It consisted of nine one-day meetings, one meeting on each of the above subjects. Notes for each meeting were prepared specially to suit the particular needs of the corporation, and illustrated with cases taken from its experience. Speakers were selected for each meeting, both from inside and outside the corporation. Next, a number of projects were selected to give to the course members. Each project was concerned with studying some aspect of the corporation's *existing* problems, objectives, systems, or information. They included:

> The information needs to be supplied by the camera parts-numbering system.
> The scope for film stock reduction.
> Key decisions analysis for the production manager.
> Analysis of the amount and effect of systems changes made during programming the "multibranch" customer invoicing project.
> Improvement of accuracy by foreman in the "shopfloor data-capture" system.
> A "dictionary" for use by management and foreman, describing the contents of the present data bank.

This "course design" stage took another three weeks.

**iv.   Running the course.** The top management of the corporation, advised by the course leader, selected 24 course members from within the firm. They were formed into two groups of 12. The course was thus divided into two streams, each group having the full, nine weekly meetings, but on a separate day of the week.

An important point is that the "effective computer" course was given to mixed groups of management and computer experts. This approach did incalculable good in breaking down the "invisible" barrier between them. It did, however, necessitate choosing subjects for each meeting which had interest and value for both user and expert. Thus program and file structure, whose study would have met a clear need only of the computer department, was not included in the syllabus.

This stage of the project lasted nine weeks. During this time, course members each devoted, on average, 12 days to the course, attending the meetings (about a half-day for each) and carrying out their projects, as individuals or in groups of two or three. Between meetings, the leader worked with the project groups.

It can be seen from the above that this firm's "effective computer" course occupied the course leader for 16 weeks and involved the 24 course members for 12 days, each spread over 9 weeks. The benefits from the course marked a turning point in the use of computers by the company, however, and included the following:

SHORT-TERM BENEFITS

It is typical of this form of training that the "projects" carried out by the course members produce immediate benefits. For example, the project on shopfloor data capture showed that 11 per cent of computer input documents contained errors. By training foreman and machine operators, redesigning the input documents, and removing certain unnecessary input fields, errors were reduced to 0.7 per cent. This allowed the complete removal of a data control section comprising 12 clerks, whose sole job had been to study these input documents and correct errors before they got to the computer.

LONGER-TERM BENEFITS

The major benefits arise in the longer term. In this case, the course led to:

> The formation of a computer task force, following the principles described in Part 2 of this book, but differing considerably in detail because they were conceived and designed by the corporation itself. The running of further in-house training in the computer department itself, covering program and file structure; the reduction of computer program running times; and the facilitation of program changes and rewrites.
>
> The quantification of benefits achieved by the corporation and attributable to the computer. Such quantification was previously thought to be impossible. Its achievement altered the firm's attitude toward the computer from the negative one of "unavoidable overhead" to a positive one of an "aid to management." This positive attitude led directly to participation in computer projects by the user.

The general benefits to be expected from this approach are:

> The *corporation*, not a particular individual, becomes the consumer of training.
>
> The course objectives are defined simply as "to assist managers and computer specialists to do their jobs better." The course concentrates on the actual problems facing them at the moment.

Our experience with this form of training leads us to define the following essential requirements:

  i.   The courses are conducted on the corporation's premises.
  ii.  The involvement and commitment of the firm's senior executives, including the chief executive, are essential.
  iii. An important feature of the course, which occupies half the time of course members, is the exacting individual project work. This culminates in a written report and oral presentation of the summary of the written paper to a panel of directors.
  iv.  The course syllabus program, course notes, and the contents of the course discussions must be tailor-made to meet the company's specific training needs.

v.   The course leader must be a professionally competent outsider, i.e., an executive from another firm, a consultant, a member of a training institution, etc.

vi.  The course meetings must be highly participatory. Principles and alternative theories and approaches must always be presented undogmatically as a basis for discussion.

## PERCEPTIVE USE OF OUTSIDE COURSES

All too often, we find that training budgets are wastefully used because men sent to outside courses are not given a very thorough critical appraisal of the relevance of the course.

▶ A warehouse group identified the need for training two systems analysts, but did not have the resources or time to undertake the training internally. After consulting the British Institute of Management they obtained course brochures from several reputable training centers. Prima facie, one management center's three-week course was the most appropriate. However, they did not make the mistake of blindly booking course places; instead the computer manager visited the center, interviewed the staff, and asked questions such as:

How long has the management center been in existence and what is the total range of courses provided?

What is the practical experience (management, professional, computer work, computer consultancy) of the tutorial staff who would teach our men?

What is the balance of tutorial techniques (cases, lecture discussions, practical projects)?

What are the teaching facilities (quality of lecture rooms, backup size of library and qualified "intelligence" staff, availability of a computer terminal for demonstrations, running programs and simulation exercises)?

What notes, textbooks, etc. are provided for permanent reference by delegates?

How many trainee systems analysts attend each course?

Can we see the delegate list for recent courses to note the past clients? What are the qualifications and requirements for acceptance?

If necessary, can you provide references of satisfied past clients?

What preliminary reading and preparation would be useful?

After the course do you give advice on the "back home" problems?

What are the administrative arrangements (costs and what is included, meals, hotels, and the like)?

Only when the computer manager was thoroughly satisfied with the answers did he make reservations. Compared with the casual way in which many firms book training course places this may seem an overrigorous approach. But the computer manager knew that far more was at stake than the fees involved, and he recognized that an outside training course is really only effective when it is run "in partnership" and with full mutual understanding of needs and purpose between client and trainees.

When the trainee systems analysts returned to their company, each man was asked to prepare a brief report summarizing what he had learned—and to give his frank assessment of the course and its strengths and weaknesses, and his recommendation whether future trainee analysts should be sent to the same management center for training. The computer manager also interviewed the men to obtain a more informal appraisal. However, his final judgment was reserved until he observed the men doing practical systems analysis work for him.

# Selecting a computer improvement strategy

Earlier in this book (Part 2), we gave a step-by-step description of the identification of computer contributions in the key result areas of the business (the "effective computer"); also, a similar description (Part 3) of the improvement of the internal efficiency of the computer department itself, which is possible through a management by objectives approach. This follows the logical sequence: "Do not waste time and effort on the computer department itself until you've checked that it is doing the right things from the business viewpoint. Otherwise, you might improve things which should not exist at all."

In real life, however, different change sequences may be required, even though the ultimate goal—an effective computer in the business sense and an efficient computer department—is the same. In selecting a computer strategy, one should consider not only human factors but also issues such as:

## STARTING AT THE TOP

Although logically preferable, this may prove difficult if top management is thoroughly frustrated by the present performance of the computer and has little confidence in the specialist staff. When pressed to state what their key result areas are and how they see the important business problems, they may become defensive because they do not know. The general level of planning and control may be so primitive that it would be naive to computerize the systems as they stand. The computer specialists may have been very successful in simple administrative applications, but it is dangerous to assume they have acquired the experience and business know-how to work on strategic management problems.

Top management may be faced with an overwhelming workload

arising from other matters, and simply may not have the time in the short term to give to a new project.

STARTING IN THE COMPUTER DEPARTMENT

This may enable existing promises and commitments to be fulfilled quickly and economically, and thus build up management confidence. Moreover, freed from short-term operational problems, the computer staff will have time to concentrate on business improvement opportunities. However, if the applications originally selected were insignificant or basically un-economical, major effort within the computer department alone can be largely self-defeating.

A PARALLEL ATTACK

Sometimes it is possible to do some work on the important areas in the computer department itself in parallel with a modest "effective computer" exercise in a selected business area. Obviously, there can be no "one right way" and it is always advisable to make a thorough initial survey of the problems and opportunities to select the right sequence and mix of improvement objectives.

The general trend is clear: in the 'sixties, the computer proved itself mainly in paperwork automation. The vast majority of existing computer applications started in information areas formerly serviced by account-ants—general accounting, payroll, sales order invoicing—and to a lesser extent in stock control, production control and marketing/sales analyses. *They replaced existing systems.* In the 'seventies, the computer will prove itself in wider managerial uses. It will help management improve the performance of the business by doing work that *has not previously been evolved into a system.* We can anticipate that by the end of the decade these new systems will account for half the total applications.

**References**

1. *Computers, Managers and Society*, Penguin Books, 1969.
2. A. Mant, *The Experienced Manager*, British Institute of Management.
3. John Gardner, *Self-Renewal: The Individual and the Innovative Society*, colophon edition, Harper and Row, 1965, pp. 78–9.
4. Abraham Maslow, *Motivation and Personality*, Harper and Row, New York, 1954.
5. Frederick Herzberg, *Work and the Nature of Man*, World Publishing Company, 1966.
6. McGraw-Hill, 1960.
7. Prepared by M. Smith of the Urwick Group Behavioral Science Unit.
8. Prepared with advice from John Lloyd, Director, Urwick Orr and Partners (UK) Ltd.

# Part 5
# Can *your* computer be more effective?

## Whose responsibility?

Only with top management leadership and example will a critical examination of the role of the computer, and any subsequent action, be of the right quality. Insisting on *results* from the computer, personal involvement in setting out the objectives and criteria for performance, creating an organizational climate in which constructive change is facilitated, and reviewing progress in a disciplined way—all these are the inescapable responsibility of top management. Of course, functional, specialist, and line managers will make their contribution. Responsibility is not *limited* to top management.

## Asking the right questions

No matter how well intentioned one may be, it usually requires a specific, self-imposed discipline to trigger action. In Figure 5.1 we list some of the key questions to be asked about the computer. The reader may care to note his answers and "first thoughts" on possible action. This analysis can be used in a variety of ways:

> The reader can make an appraisal of his own organization. The speed and, indeed, the possibility of taking the proposed actions may depend as much on the reader's ingenuity and persuasiveness as on his formal status. It will help, however, to be the chief executive!

> A group of people can work on this together by having each individual manager make his analysis, and then meet as a group to exchange opinions.

Ideally, this should be a mixed group of computer specialists and line managers. At the "opinion" stage, an outside expert may be useful to provide a comparison with other installations.

It is technically, organizationally (and, probably, politically) wrong to *overestimate* the value of this informal questioning approach. The *real purpose* is to: expose problems, create a sense of humility, and start a communication process. Thus top management can move to a stage at which it formally gets under way a planned, thorough approach to making the corporation's computer really effective on lines described in this book.

At a different level of action, this questioning is very useful as an exercise on *computer training and appreciation courses*. The book may be studied before the course starts, then each delegate can bring his completed set of questions. This provides invaluable "raw material" for discussion groups and tutorials. It is also possible to use the book and searching questions as a personal, follow-up action for students on their return home.

---

How well is the computer used in the business?

*Objectives*

Consider the original statement of objectives on which you based your decision to buy or hire a computer.

When were these objectives last reviewed critically, restated, and communicated to everyone?

Do the current objectives merely set out general statements of intent; e.g., "to improve on management information," "computerize customer accounts"?

Or do they merely concern themselves with cost savings in present administration services; e.g., "to reduce the number of clerks from x to y by z date"?

Or do they set out clear, measured objectives for improvements in areas significant for better business results?

Are these objectives the product of joint discussion between top management, computer specialists, and the operations managers who must secure the benefits?

*Policies*

Do you have policy statements in the important areas of the business and the computer to provide guidance on recurring questions; e.g., on the use of human beings on repetitive "rule following" tasks?

Are minor decisions about the computer frequently referred upward for "policy clearance"?

---

**Figure 5.1**

*Performance*

What system has been instituted to measure the extent to which your objectives are being achieved?

Can you identify measurable business results that can be attributed to the computer?

Do these results justify the costs connected with the computer?

Do computer teams feel their prime objective is to "get the job going" satisfactorily, or to get the benefits originally aimed for?

Who has the specific objective of getting these original benefits?

Are you sure that precious high-quality resources (e.g., the investment in the computer and its people) are not drifting into low-opportunity areas?

How does the use of your computer compare with the best computer installations; e.g., nonproductive computer time, programmer output, return on investment?

*Organization*

Have you considered the impact on your organization structure following the introduction of the computer; e.g., new and complex staff–line relationships, changes in nature of some operational manager responsibilities, change in balance of discretionary and nondiscretionary control, implications for "centralization" versus "decentralization" issue?

*Control*

Has the computer given managers control information on the key results they must achieve?

Is it
  Simple?
  Relevant?
  Timely?
  Acceptable?
Is there too much control information, so that perception is confused?

*Attitudes*

Do line managers and computer specialists talk to one another?

Do they listen as much as they talk?

Is there a flow of information between the two, so that a sense of common purpose and understanding is built up?

Do they feel free to approach one another with ideas and suggestions for change?

Do they consult one another on problems not strictly within their responsibility?

**Figure 5.1** *(contd)*

Do they have enough information, written and oral, to know how they are getting on and how the business is shaping overall?

Are the mistakes inevitable in developing a new computer project treated as "crimes" or as opportunities to learn together?

*Management development*

Do you have a regular manager performance and potential review program?

What practical use do you make of reviews?

Do you prepare for your managers a training plan for the computer?

Who creates it?
    Executive management?
    Computer management?
    Both?

Is it difficult to fill key management posts when they become vacant?

Do you have a company succession plan?

Is there a planned interchange between line management and computer management?

Do top managers take time to discuss promising young men and problems?

Are you "hoarding" talent that could, in the interest of man and company, be better used elsewhere?

Does your salary system attract and hold the right quality and number of managers and computer personnel?

Does it reward managers in relation to their potential and the results they achieve?

*How well is the computer department managed?*

Is there a written set of objectives for the computer department that interlock with company objectives?

Is each person in the department really clear about:
    The key results he must achieve?
    The performance standards and criteria by which he will be judged?
    The control information he receives to monitor progress?
    The limits of his authority?

Is there an effective control system within the department; e.g., are projects met on time and budgeted project costs kept?

Are people properly trained and motivated to work individually and in task forces?

Is the department managed mainly on a "fire fighting" crisis basis? (Think carefully about this: What plans were made last year? Do things go according to plan? What upsets these plans? Do your project leaders and experts believe in planning?)

**Figure 5.1** *(contd)*

What is the productive utilization of your equipment; i.e., the percentage of productive time? And the number of shifts operated? Are you satisfied with this utilization: In particular, is there an attitude favoring the maximum use of the machine, or do you attempt to measure utilization/work-done ratios?

Did the costs of data processing increase during the past two years? Did you allow for this increase in your original project plan, and was it justified by business improvements?

Are project leaders allowed to leave projects before the terms of reference are achieved?

Do you set project objectives for:
    Benefits?
    System outputs?
    Time?
    Cost?

Is each of these objectives reviewed at least quarterly? Do the computer department/senior management/project leaders behave as though the information available at the commencement of projects is sufficient to set realistic objectives in each of the above categories? What degree of time and cost escalation or shortfall of benefits and system outputs took place on projects completed last year?

    Have you developed effective countermeasures against:
        Industrial action/physical attack that may put the computer out of action?
        Penetration of the computer system by competitors or other outsiders?
        Fraudulent operation of the computer system?
    (Have you studied this problem?)

**Figure 5.1** (contd)

# Benefits

The reward for undertaking a systematic approach to managing the computer invariably includes:

A system for obtaining payoff from computers; in particular, the formulation of plans and policies for employing frequently misused computer resources and potential to secure profit improvements for the business.

The end of disappointment and doubt concerning the contribution of the computer to the business, and the substitution of clear, measured justifications to which all managers subscribe, with the assurance that computing power *is* concentrated on the key needs of the business.

A constructive team effort between computer specialists and executive managers; in place of any atmosphere of separatism, mistrust, "going it alone," etc.

Improved efficiency within the computer department itself (such as cost reduction, project control, output quality, confidence and respect of users), including the development of a "management climate" that secures the full motivation, commitment, and enthusiasm of all the "knowledge workers" in the department.

Continuing on-the-job computer training and development for all managers and computer experts alike, leading to a thorough appreciation by all key people of the proper role of the computer in the organization.

# Appendix 1
# What do businessmen need to know about the computer?

## The basic facts

Most people tend to look upon the computer as a "black box," full of mysteries and capable of assuming a mind of its own. In fact, the computer is none of these things and its powers can be easily understood. Basically, the machine consists of only five elements, as illustrated in Figure A1.1.

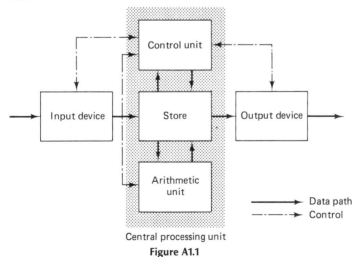

Central processing unit

**Figure A1.1**

This appendix is Part 2 of *Computers in Business—101 Points for Managers*, and is used by kind permission of the National Computing Centre Ltd and the BBC.

### Input devices

These are the means by which instructions to operate on data, or the data itself, are transferred to the computer. The most common methods of input are punched cards and punched paper tape, but many others have been developed.

### Output devices

These are the means by which the computer communicates the results of its processing to the outside world. The main device used to output information is the line printer; some models are capable of printing up to 2,000 lines per minute.

### Storage

The internal store of the computer is the part of the machine in which the program of instructions is kept and to which data is passed by the input devices. One can visualize the internal store as a series of pigeon-holes, into each of which a piece of data (a number or a character) can be placed (stored). The internal store is the most expensive part of the modern computer, and so, for economic reasons, another kind of storage is used, which is known as an auxiliary or backing store.

Backing storage normally holds files and other information not immediately required by the program. Backing-storage devices are available in a number of forms; the choice is usually a compromise between operating requirements and costs. The commonest and cheapest form is the magnetic tape on which information is stored serially and which is read by a device similar to a domestic tape recorder. Because information is stored serially, it may be necessary to read a full tape to reach a piece of information at the end of it. Magnetic tapes are normally removed after processing and stored for use at a later date.

Another common backing-storage device is the magnetic disk, which looks like a smooth gramophone record with a moving reading head. The use of single or multiple disks allows much faster access to information than magnetic tape, but disks are more expensive.

### The arithmetic unit

This is the most important part of the computer, but basically it can only do five things:

Add
Subtract
Multiply
Divide
Compare

It is powerful because of the speed with which it carries out the calculations—many hundreds in a thousandth of a second.

### The control unit

This interprets the instructions in the program and activates the input, storage, arithmetic, and output units, as the program requires.

The flow of data is from the input device into internal store (and onto backing store if required); from internal store in and out of the arithmetic unit, then out to the output device. Normally, the control, internal storage, and arithmetic units are housed in the same cabinet, known as the central processing unit; the input, output, and backing-storage devices are known as peripheral equipment.

To sum up, therefore, the computer is not a mysterious device. It consists of five parts and can only perform five basic functions. The power of the machine lies in its speed, and in the hands of the programmers who devise the schedule of instructions it must follow. The computer can have no mind of its own; it is controlled by its programmers who, in turn, are controlled by the management of the environment in which they find themselves. The computer does not control; it is controlled by management.

## Hardware

All the electronic and electromechanical devices described in the last section are known as the hardware of computing. The combination of basic units selected by the computer user to fulfill his processing requirements is known as a configuration. A typical configuration might be as shown in Figure A1.2.

This shows the central processing unit, six magnetic tape units for backing storage, two card readers for input, two line printers for output, and a console, which allows processing to be initiated, machine usage to be recorded, malfunctions to be indicated, and general communication between the operator and the machine.

The user may initially purchase a small configuration and later increase

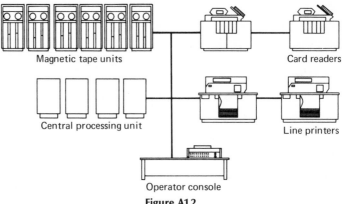

Magnetic tape units                                          Card readers

Central processing unit

Line printers

Operator console

**Figure A1.2**

its size by adding more peripheral equipment or more internal storage as his processing requirements grow. He may, of course, also make use of a computer service bureau, either by simply delivering his work to the bureau or by making use of a "remote terminal." This device, bought or rented, is connected through the telephone system to the central bureau machine. The terminal can be a simple, electric typewriterlike device, a "visual display unit" with TV-like screen, or a small computer with card or paper-tape reader and printer of its own.

During the 'sixties, the available computing power for a given expenditure increased by as much as a thousand times. It is unlikely that development will continue at this rate, but there is little doubt that the cost of the electronic computing elements will continue to fall. But already, the remaining mechanical components (printers, magnetic tape drives, etc.) are proving limiting factors in cost and space reduction.

## Software

The hardware described in the previous section cannot by itself display any form of initiative, and must be "programmed" to perform specific tasks. A program may be defined as a set of instructions to the computer that states precisely how a particular processing task is to be performed.

The first main stage in preparing a computer program is to identify the nature of the problem to be tackled, by examining input, file information, and output. After problem definition, the next stage is that of developing a solution—devising the broad processing steps that have to be taken before input becomes output. A commonly accepted and suitable technique for recording these steps is the flowchart. Figure A1.3 shows a typical system flowchart for a sales invoicing application.

A programmer would take each of the boxes of this flowchart and break it down into a further series of flowcharts. From these program flowcharts, he would then write the necessary program instructions. The basic levels of programming are often referred to as "machine coding" or "assembly level" or "low-level programming." With this, each instruction written by the programmer corresponds with one of the basic functions of the computer, such as "add," "subtract," or "store."

Although this method is still used for special work, it is being superseded for general commercial use by the "high-level languages." At this level, the programmer writes instructions that are reasonably similar to conventional business phrases, and the translation to the detail coding is carried out by the computer itself. One instruction in a high-level language could result in, perhaps, 40 instructions eventually carried out by the computer.

In general, any collection of programs that turn the computer into an effective tool is termed the "software." But the term is often more specifically used to describe the general-purpose programs supplied by a computer manufacturer or specialist supplier, as opposed to the programs written by a computer user for his own purposes.

## Typical invoicing system flowchart

1.  The first program transfers the data onto a magnetic tape, having first checked that the data is correct—that the account number is all numeric if it is supposed to be.
2.  The second program is a sort program. It sorts the magnetic tape into product number order.
3.  Program 3 takes the sorted tape and matches it against the product master file, i.e., goes through the master file, one record after another, comparing the product numbers on each magnetic tape until equality is found. Once equality is found, relevant product information is moved onto the dispatch notes tape—e.g., product name, price.
4.  Program 4 is another sort program; it takes the dispatch notes tape (which now has product information on it) and sorts it into customer order.
5.  Program 5 matches the dispatch note tape against the customer master file and extracts customer details—e.g., name and address, discounts, etc. After each record has been matched, the invoice value

is calculated (e.g., quantity × price − discount) and the invoice is printed.

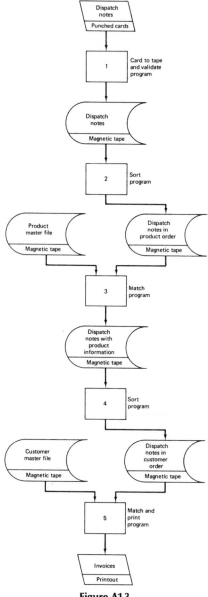

**Figure A1.3**

## The input problem

At the moment computers suffer from the limitation that input has to be presented to them in a coded form. This means that input documents have to be converted into computer-readable input. The vast majority of computer installations make use of either punched cards or punched paper tape as input media; key punches, which are similar to typewriters, are used to punch holes into long strips of paper tape or into orthodox punched cards. This is called data preparation. Considerable attention has to be paid to ensure that what has been punched is correct, because the computer is limited in its ability to determine which input data are "clean." Thus a verification stage is introduced into the data-preparation cycle. The punched cards (or tape) are fed into a more sophisticated punch, called a verifier, and repunched. Where a discrepancy occurs, the verifier locks, and a decision is taken as to what the correct version should be. The verified card (or tape) then becomes the input to the computer. Two factors influence the efficiency of this routine, dull operation.

### 1. The need for well-trained punch operators

Operators need to be trained to achieve a high, consistent work standard with as few errors as possible. Such training is expensive and takes a long time.

### 2. The need for good document design

A prerequisite for an efficient punching operation is the use of standard documents on which information to be punched is logically ordered. In recent years considerable advances have been made in the development of input devices that will accept handwritten or typewritten documents. In removing the need for data preparation, such advances will alleviate some of the problems, but a cheap solution has not yet been found. It seems likely that for a number of years input will remain one of the most costly, time-consuming aspects of computer operations.

## Where do the costs lie?

The word "computer" covers a very wide range of equipment, from a small "visible-record machine" or "minicomputer" to a monstrous tele-processing, multiprogramming giant. The median of the price distribution for computers has shifted from about $240,000 in the early 'sixties to about $48,000 in current purchasing. At the end of 1970, about 65 per cent of all computers sold in the UK were valued at less than $48,000.

For the service bureau user, facilities can be obtained from as little as $24 a week, and $2,400 a year can buy some quite useful facilities for a small business.

The costs of any proposed system lie normally in three categories.

## Development

These costs include salaries and overhead for programmers and systems analysts and management and education costs. They tend to be the ones susceptible to underestimation and, therefore, should be carefully watched. In determining whether the level of development costs is acceptable, one should pay attention to application packages and co-operative developments.

## Running

These costs can be fairly accurately estimated if a computer is to be bought, and should include the capital cost of the computer and ancillary

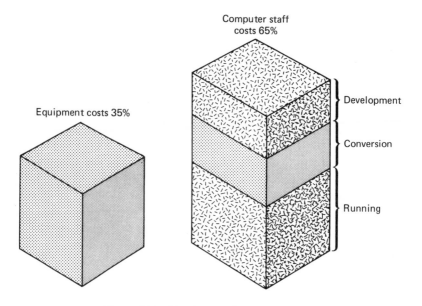

**Figure A1.4**   Distribution of computer costs.

equipment, its installation, accommodation, salaries for operating department staff, stationery supplies, and computer supplies. Obviously, it is in the area of running costs that a comparison has to be made between owning a computer and using a computer bureau.

## Conversion

This area of cost often involves spending large amounts at irregular intervals and so should be carefully watched. Many potential users budget carefully for development and running costs but forget to account for the problems of changing from one system to another.

## Using a computer: batch processing

Most computers in business organizations tackle processing sequentially —this means that records/documents are processed through the computer system in a predetermined order. This is because sequential processing can take advantage of the very low cost of magnetic tape for the storage of large files. Sequential processing means that transactions must be gathered together, sorted into the order of the file, and matched with the records on the file; these groups are called batches, and this form of processing is called batch processing.

Batch processing is the commonest method of using a computer and, perhaps, always will be. It is well suited to many data processing jobs, it lends itself to the use of control totals (i.e., batches can be controlled as they pass through the system) and other error procedures, and it involves the least expensive configurations of equipment.

## Using a computer: real-time processing

While needing information to be as current as possible at the time of a deadline, e.g., month end for a ledger, most clerical operations do not need current information all the time. For example, there is no need to have every employee's earnings calculated at every point in time during a pay period. However, in certain circumstances, the opposite applies— the manufacturer needs to know the state of his stocks; the airline must know the availability of seats on a particular flight; a bank clerk may need to check an account balance when a customer inquires, or when a check is to be paid. This need for access to current information is common to many business situations; if the computer is to be used, it must be able to cope with the need.

Sequential or batch processing, however, as described in the previous section, does not allow this facility. Records are processed in order, starting at the first and finishing with the last; this militates against access to any record as and when required; and in any case, magnetic tapes tend to be taken off the tape handler as soon as they have been brought up to date, so that they are not available for *ad hoc* inquiries. Thus, to meet the need for *current* information demands, a more complex, nonsequential method of processing has been devised. It is called real-time processing— this means that processing takes place in the time available to make decisions that affect events, e.g., the time available while the customer waits, or the production equipment is waiting between jobs. This type of processing is also sometimes referred to as on-line or conversational processing.

A real-time system makes a number of demands on the computer user in terms of equipment. For example, there is an unavoidable need for random access storage (i.e., storage devices that offer the facility of finding any piece of information in approximately the same time interval); there is need for on-line equipment as discussed in the next section; if the inquirer is located at some distance from the computer, data transmission facilities will be required, i.e., being able to transmit information along telephone lines or by direct cable connection.

It will be clear from what has been said that real-time processing is expensive, and because of its complexity creates problems of reliability and recovery from error.

## Using a computer: on-line processing

A piece of equipment that is described as on-line operates under the direct control of the central processing unit. On-line equipment can be located in the same place as the central processing unit or in a remote place. But generally, when people speak of on-line processing, they refer to processing via a terminal remote from the computer. This terminal can be in various forms. It could be a visual display unit, which is like a television screen with a keyboard—input is passed to the computer by keying it in on the keyboard, and output from the computer is displayed on the screen—or it could be a teletypewriter, which is similar to an ordinary typewriter, and is used for keying input into the computer and for printing output received from the computer.

A system that uses such equipment is described as an on-line processing system and normally works in real-time, as described in the previous section. However, it is possible to use on-line equipment for batch processing also, and this is usually known as remote batch processing or remote job entry. This means that a central computer is being used to service a remote input location; input data, usually in the form of paper tape, are transmitted in batches from a remote location, processed by the central computer, and the output is returned by the data transmission system to the remote location.

## Using a computer: time sharing

All real-time computer systems provide a service to many independent users within an organization and are, therefore, time-sharing or time-shared systems; that is, they share their resources among randomly occurring requests. Time sharing is widely used to describe systems that serve, apparently simultaneously, a large number of users.

The time-shared system can serve many users in one organization and so, naturally, can be used to serve one user in multiple organizations. A time-sharing operation should reduce costs because all the users are sharing one machine, and should make greater computer power available to those users because by sharing they can pay for a large, powerful computer, which could offer more advanced facilities than a small machine, that each independently could afford.

# Appendix 2
# Further study

## Films

**Management by objectives with John Humble.** An EMI series of six 30-minute color films with supplementary study material.

**Who needs the computer?** An EMI 12-minute color film. Technical adviser: Kit Grindley.

**Information systems.** A 30-minute case history color film with associated 30-minute discussion film featuring Isaac Auerbach, president of the Auerbach Corporation. These films are in the BNA Humble "Management Practice" series.

These films are available through

> EMI Special Films Unit
> Dean House
> 7, Soho Square
> London W1V 5FA
> England.

for the UK and distribution outside North America, and

> BNA Films
> 5615 Fishers Lane
> Rockville
> Maryland, USA 20852.

for the United States and Canada.

**Computers in Business.** Film copies of nine BBC television programs are available from

The Central Film Library
Government Buildings
Bromyard Avenue
London W3
England.

## Books

*Computer Users' Year Book*, published each June, available from Dept. C, 18 Queen's Road, Brighton, Sussex, England.
*Computers in Business*, BBC Publications, London, 1971.
*Computers in Central Government Ten Years Ahead*, HMSO, London, 1971.
Daniels, A., and Yeats, P., *Basic Training in Systems Analysis*, National Computing Centre, London, 1969.
Employment and Productivity Department of Joint Committee of Industrial Training Boards. *The Training of the Systems Analysts (Commercial)*, HMSO, London, 1969.
Fletcher, A. (editor), *Computer Science for Management*, Business Books, London, 1967.
Harper, R. J., *Data Processing Managers*, Lyon, Grant and Green, (Administrative Staff College), 1967.
Hollingdale, S. H., and Toothill, G. C., *Electronic Computers*, Penguin Books, London, 1965.
Humble, J. W., *Improving Business Results*, McGraw-Hill, London and New York, for Management Centre/Europe, Brussels, 1965.
————, *Management by Objectives*, Management Publications for British Institute of Management, London, 1972.
————, *Management by Objectives in Action*, McGraw-Hill, London, 1970.
London, K., *Introduction to Computers*, Faber, London, 1968.
Losty, P. A., *Effective Use of Computers in Business*, Cassell, London, 1969.
McRae, T. W. (editor), *Management Information Systems*, Penguin Modern Management Readings, Penguin Books, London, 1971.
*Computers, Planning and Personnel Management*, Mumford, Enid, Institute of Personnel Management, London, 1969.
National Computing Centre, *A System Documented*, London, 1971.
————, *Computer-Aided Production Control*, 1972 edition.
————, *Computers in Vehicle Scheduling*, 1969.

National Computing Centre, *Economic Evaluation of Computer-Based Systems* (3 vols.), 1971.

————, *Computer Personnel Selection:*
>    1. *Systems Analysts*, 1970.
>    2. *Programmers*, 1972.

————, *Systems Documentation Manual*, 1970.

————, *The Impact of Computer Techniques on Road Transport Planning*, 1970.

————, *Using Computers—A Guide for the Manager*, 1971. An extension of and complementary to *Computers in Business—101 Points for Managers*.

————, *Working with Computers*, 1970.

Phillips, G. M., and Taylor, P. J., *Computers*, Methuen, London, 1969.

Sanderson, P. C., *Computers for Management*, Pan Books, London, 1969.

Stewart, Rosemary, *How Computers Affect Management*, Macmillan, London, 1971.

Sturt, H. and Yearsley, R., *Computers for Management*, Heinemann, London, 1969.

Summersbee, S., *Computer Case Histories*, Machinery Publishing, Brighton, 1970.

Tatham, L., *The Use of Computers for Profit*, McGraw-Hill, London, 1970.

Tomlin, R., *Managing the Introduction of Computer Systems*, McGraw-Hill, New York and London, 1970.

Willie, Edgar, *The Computer in Personnel Work*, Institute of Personnel Management, London, 1966.

## Computer surveys

*Analysis of Computer Usage in the U.K. in 1971: Factfinder 10*. By the National Computing Centre, London, 1972, 72 pp.

*U.K. Computer Industry Trends 1970 to 1980: Implications for DP Users and the Service Industry*.
>    By The Hoskyns Group, London, October 1969, 21 pp.

*Achieving Computer Profitability: A Survey of Current Practice in 102 Companies*.
>    By H. Johannsen and S. Birch, London, British Institute of Management Surveys and Publications Department, 1971, 43 pp. (Management Survey Report No. 1).

*A Survey of the Computer Industry*.
>    Supplement to *The Economist*, February 27, 1971, 39 pp.

*Unlocking the Computer's Profit Potential. A Research Report to Management.*

By McKinsey and Company, New York, 1968, 38 pp.

*The Computer Profit Drain. A Research Study on Computer Utilization in the United States.*

By A. T. Kearney and Company, London, October 1970, 18 pp.

## Seminars

Appreciation seminars on *The Effective Computer* are run in various parts of the world. For latest schedule, contact

> Kit Grindley or John Humble
> The Urwick Group
> 50 Doughty Street,
> London WCN 2LS
> England.

# Index

## DATE DUE

| | | | |
|---|---|---|---|
| DEC 14 78 | | | |
| NO 21 '82 | | | |
| NOV 15 83 | | | |
| DEC 2 '83 | | | |
| DE 16 '83 | | | |
| AP 4 '88 | | | |
| | | | |
| | | | |
| | | | |
| | | | |
| | | | |
| | | | |
| | | | |
| | | | |
| | | | |
| | | | |